Five Steps

to

Forgiveness

✳

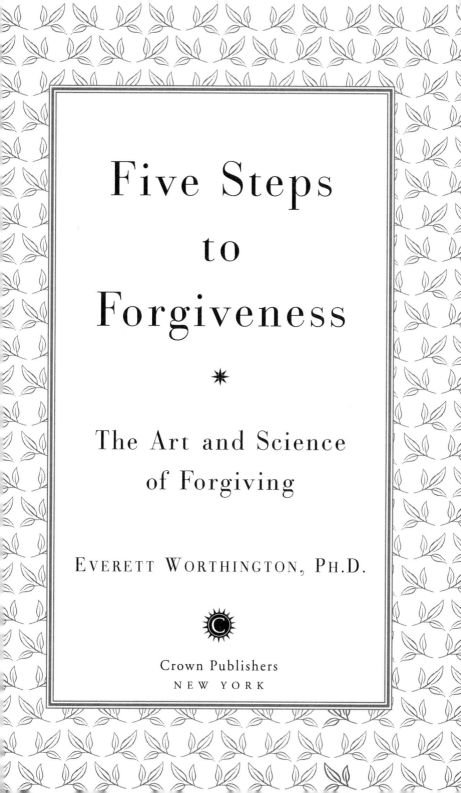

Five Steps
to
Forgiveness

*

The Art and Science
of Forgiving

E VERETT W ORTHINGTON, P H.D.

Crown Publishers
NEW YORK

Copyright © 2001 by Everett L. Worthington, Jr., Ph.D.

Published by Crown Publishers, New York, New York.
Member of the Crown Publishing Group.

Random House, Inc. New York, Toronto, London, Sydney, Auckland
www.randomhouse.com

CROWN is a trademark and the Crown colophon is a registered trademark of
Random House, Inc.

Printed in the United States of America

Design by Lynne Amft

Library of Congress Cataloging-in-Publication Data
Worthington, Everett L., 1946–
Five steps to forgiveness : the art and science of forgiving /
Everett Worthington.—1st ed.
1. Forgiveness.   2. Reconciliation.   I. Title.
BF637.F67 W67 2001
155.9'2—dc21   2001028367

ISBN 0-609-60918-1

10 9 8 7 6 5 4 3 2 1

First Edition

In memory of
FRANCES MCNEILL WORTHINGTON

CONTENTS

✳

PREFACE

Chances are, you've experienced some transgressions from well-meaning helpers, parents who "know what's good for you," oblivious lovers and friends, stressed-out caretakers, children who disappoint, bosses who have their own agenda, or simply people with a mean streak. Humans get hurt or offended. That's part of being human.

Chances are also high that with at least one of those transgressions you worried it around, like an aching tooth you can't stop exploring with your tongue. Perhaps you sometimes catch the bitterness in your tone of voice. Maybe you've taken petty revenge and hate yourself for it. Perhaps you plot revenge on a larger scale and don't like the direction your mind has been working in. You're stuck.

Perhaps the problem occurred in the past. Maybe you're divorced and can't get beyond the resentment. Or maybe your father died without giving you the chance to make things right with him. You want to forgive. You need to forgive.

Perhaps you're in an ongoing relationship that has gone sour— at home, at work, or with a romantic partner. You've invested in that relationship and don't want to give it up. You want to reconcile. But how?

This book is for you. My colleagues and I have conducted research for years on how people can forgive and, if they wish, work toward reconciliation. We have studied people in the laboratory using experiments on how people talk about transgressions. We have studied how people respond physiologically to transgression and have seen how they calm down when they forgive. We have measured stress hormones in people's saliva. In addition, we have done numerous groups to help individuals forgive and couples reconcile after they forgive each other. I have distilled our research into a five-step model for how to forgive, which I call the Pyramid Model to REACH Forgiveness. I have also boiled down our thinking about reconciling to a four-step Bridge to Reconciliation. I've been delighted and amazed at how many have learned to apply these models to forgive and reconcile.

Forgiving is never as simple as merely applying five steps in thirty minutes and *poof!* instant forgiveness. That trivializes a serious and personal experience.

Reconciliation between two parties in conflict is even more complicated. Each person can run aground on the rocks of self-protection and good intentions.

Nevertheless, you can remember the five steps you need to forgive and the four steps you need to reconcile. In this book, I suggest concrete ways to apply the steps. I show you how to get back on track after temporary setbacks.

Forgiveness and reconciliation are not simple. They require courage, commitment, and conscious effort. But if you are willing, there are great treasures to be given—and yes, sometimes even received—when you forgive and try to reconcile. I wish you great success in applying these ideas.

✳

Why Forgive?

Like a bee, we distill poison from honey for our self-defense—what happens to the bee if it uses its sting is well known.

—DAG HAMMARSKJÖLD

On New Year's Eve in 1995, my mother was murdered in her home by a young burglar. It has affected me as much as any event ever has, and even today the pain still occasionally bobs to the emotional surface.

When I received the call from Mike, my brother, on New Year's morning, I was stunned. "Something terrible has happened," he said. "Mama's been murdered. There was blood on the carpet, the walls. . . ."

As I got ready to drive from Richmond to Knoxville with my sister, Kathy, and her husband, Damian, I threw clothes in a suitcase, hustling furiously to and fro, numbing my feelings with the narcotic of action. After I was packed, I sat at the table. I heard Kirby, my wife, reading to teenage Becca the children's stories that Grandma used to read her. Preteen Katy Anna walked by, face wet with tears. I reached out to comfort her. Her hug broke through my defenses, and I wept.

On the drive to Knoxville, Kathy and I replayed many of the good times and bad with my mother. I remembered when I had done a radio call-in show with a station in Knoxville only months before. At the end of the hour, the interviewer said, "We have time for one more call, and I think this is a special one. Go ahead." I then heard the slow, soft east Tennessee voice of my mother. "Sonny"—she drawled my nickname through four diphthongs—"I've been listening to you for the last hour. I wanted you to know. You're a good boy, Sonny." I was forty-nine at the time.

Mama was a comfortable grandmother, enfolding my children in her arms, hugging them to her soft and cuddly body. She liked to sing to my kids. She read books, bought toys Kirby and I couldn't afford, and had a giant stash of M&M's and sweet breakfast cereal that kept our kids on a sugar kick throughout our visits. Since my dad had died of cancer five years before, Mama seemed more vulnerable.

Now she was gone. I wouldn't feel her arms again. I wouldn't hear the music of her east Tennessee mountain drawl. My mind could understand the loss, but my heart would simply not accept it.

THE CROWBAR

After arriving in Knoxville, my brother, my sister, and I sat in Mike's back room that night amid the seventeen loaves of bread, twenty pies, and five plates of cold cuts that neighbors and friends had provided out of their generosity. We began to talk about the details of the murder, which we knew only because Mike had walked in on Mama's body. "I called Mama all morning to wish her a happy New Year," said Mike. "When she didn't answer, I got worried. I thought she might have fallen."

Mike had bundled eight-year-old David into the car and chugged over to the house. "I opened the front door with my key. When I stepped into the living room, I couldn't believe the mess. I stumbled with David at my side toward the hall. As I stepped into the hall, I saw the blood-splattered wall. Then her body.

"I slapped my hand over David's eyes and walked out to phone the police." The violence in the house, the blood, and the position of Mama's body made it clear she was dead.

The Baseball Bat

In Mike's back room, he told us the facts the police had shared. Apparently a burglary had gone awry. The police suspected that two youths were involved.

Mama had been struck three times with a crowbar. Blood was everywhere—on the door, on the walls, soaked through the carpet. The assailant had also violated her with a wine bottle and then completely trashed the house. All mirrors and every reflecting surface in the house were ruined.

Rage spewed forth. I heard myself say, "I'd like to have him alone in a room with a baseball bat for thirty minutes. I'd beat his brains out."

Kathy said, "I'd just take ten minutes."

Mike added, "I'd take two hours, so that it would last a long time."

We were furious.

That night, sleep was impossible. I roamed my room. I stormed about, rehearsing scenes of violence and anger, replaying the death scene as I imagined it in the late-show reruns of my mind, seeing the blood in my mind's eye.

I confess that during most of that night, forgiveness never entered my mind. But as I wrestled the covers and paced a path in the carpet, I began to ask myself questions. Could I forgive? Is it good to forgive? What if the police caught the youths involved? Would I wish upon the accomplice and murderer the death penalty? I was eyeball to eyeball with my convictions—carefully thought out in times unclouded by emotion. But the impact of the death and the horror of my imagining what my mother might have experienced was an in-your-face confrontation. It rocked my sense of identity. I thought I knew my own character. Yet someone once said, "Character is who we are when no one is looking." Well, who was I in that bedroom when no one was looking?

> *Yet someone once said, "Character is who we are when no one is looking." Well, who was I in that bedroom when no one was looking?*

Self-Searching

SO, WHO WAS I?

I was a Christian. Was it wrong for me to indulge my rage? Was it wrong to want both the law and God to punish those youths? Christianity is the cross where justice and mercy intersect. At that moment, I was happy to seek justice, even the wild vigilante justice of raw revenge. I wanted my hands on that murderer. I did not even want to consider mercy.

I was a counseling psychologist. I had seen people deny experiences, stuff their worst feelings inside. Was it wrong to consider forgiveness while I was so angry and sad? I knew that if I sought too quick a resolution to trauma by denying anger, fear, and sadness, I could arrest grieving. Was it wrong to try to calm my anger when feeling intense, legitimate anger was normal? But I was in a quandary. I didn't want to deny my negative feelings, but I also knew that denying my positive side, my morals and my self-control, was just as bad. I dared not simply rage. Not only psychology but also Mama had taught me that.

I was a researcher who, ironically, studied forgiveness.[1] I had read philosophical, religious, devotional, and literary accounts of forgiveness. I had pored over psychological studies of forgiveness. Yet all day, I had not thought the word *forgiveness.* Perhaps I heard the whisper of the word *forgiveness* at the door of consciousness, but each time I kicked the door shut.

I had successfully helped numerous couples and individuals to forgive. My colleagues and I had developed an intervention that helped people forgive if they wanted to forgive. We had studied it scientifically. I had poured much of my professional and personal life into forgiveness. I knew forgiveness might be possible, but did I really want to forgive?

QUESTIONS

The poignant questions that pierced my heart were these: For whom was my life's work of teaching to forgive? Was it for other people but not for me? Or did that forgiveness, which we claimed was accessible to anyone, include me too?

> *The poignant questions that pierced my heart were these: For whom was my life's work of teaching to forgive? Was it for other people but not for me? Or did that forgiveness, which we claimed was accessible to anyone, include me too?*

Forgiveness requires both letting go and pulling toward. A forgiver must be motivated to release the resentment, hatred, and bitterness of unforgiveness. A forgiver releases the desire to avoid or seek revenge against the perpetrator. But the act of pulling toward—of reaching out toward the transgressor—is sharper. It pricks the heart. A forgiver replaces unforgiveness with a sense of nonpossessive love and wishing the perpetrator well. A forgiver could even enter a relationship with the perpetrator if it was safe, prudent, and possible to do so. Forgiveness means giving a gift that embodies freedom and love. Should I offer this gift? Should I forgive?

The Great Debate

Don't You Dare Forgive

I had heard many arguments against forgiveness before. "If you forgive, it will take away your motivation to catch the perpetrator. Forgiveness obstructs justice." Yet I knew that any forgiving I could give would be *my* act, *my* gift. The justice system could consider pardon. God might someday grant divine forgiveness. Those were out of my hands. Whether I forgave or didn't, legal crime, punishment, or pardon was not at stake. The murderer should be incarcerated so that he would not kill again. To protect others from violence is simply good sense. It didn't affect whether I ought to forgive.

I had heard people argue that unforgiveness is beneficial. "Unforgiveness empowers people to do good," said a bitter man whose child had been murdered. "Because I refuse to forgive, I also help other victims of crime." Righteous anger can motivate acts of charity. Betty Williams, who won the Nobel Peace Prize, was angry about mines planted during warfare that ambushed people long after the war ceased. She organized a campaign to remove those mines. That saved lives, reduced pain. But I can be angry with HIV/AIDS and work to stamp it out without bitterness, resentment, and hostility. Righteous anger is not the same as bitter, resentful, hateful, hostile, and ruminative unforgiveness.

"If you forgive, it's cowardly," I've heard. Having faced a major issue and struggled with whether to forgive, I can't buy that. For me, to forgive was harder than to hate. It's not cowardly to want to give up the hatred that makes a person feel powerful (and wish the perpetrator were weak). It takes courage to grant a love that can help both transgressor and victim feel better as people. Take Chris Carrier, for example, whose story has been told in *Reader's Digest*.[2] I heard him when we appeared on television's *Leeza*. At ten, Chris was abducted. He was stabbed in the chest and stomach with an ice pick and shot through the temple and eye. Left for dead in a Florida swamp, he awoke later. Chris forgave the man. Then came the acid test. When Chris was an adult, he heard that the man who had done these things to him was dying. Chris comforted the man during his final days. Chris's forgiveness was refined into pure love. Was that cowardice? It is courage personified.

"It's not my place to forgive," said one man whose child had been kidnapped and murdered. "My child was harmed. She is the only one who could forgive. But she's dead and can't forgive. Murder is unforgivable." I understood his pain. I wanted to ask him, "If the murder was not also a sin against you, how can you hate? How can you be unforgiving?" It seemed to me that his child's murder had hurt him too. If he could hate, why couldn't he forgive? His forgiveness would not pardon the killer. It would not do away with all of the killer's guilt.

"Forgiveness short-circuits grief," some might worry. Yet

forgiveness does not deny that a true offense or hurt occurred. It also does not deny the pain and sadness of a true loss. In fact, forgiveness works hand in glove with grieving to help resolve grief faster and more thoroughly.

"Forgiveness is loving toward the wrongdoer but not the victim," some people argue. As Cynthia Ozick has recalled, "The rabbi said, 'Whoever is merciful to the cruel will end by being indifferent to the innocent.' Forgiveness can brutalize. . . . The face of forgiveness is mild but how stony to be slaughtered." Yet once a wrong is done to a victim, does it help the victim to seek punitive justice? If the wrong involved property, fair restitution is indeed kind. But my mother had been murdered, and no restitution could restore what the locust of death had devoured. Whether I forgave or not wouldn't affect Mama. But I could honor her memory by living out the values of love and mercy she had bequeathed to me.

You Must Forgive

I also knew some of the counterarguments made by apologists for forgiveness. I had heard three arguments that said we should forgive for our own sake.

First, "You can't hurt the perpetrator by being unforgiving, but you can set yourself free by forgiving." I had made that argument myself to psychotherapy clients and friends. It is true to some degree.

Second, "Unforgiveness is a heavy burden to carry." True. Resentment, one of the core elements of unforgiveness, is like carrying around a red-hot rock with the intention of someday throwing it back at the one who hurt you. It tires us and burns us. Who wouldn't want simply to let the rock fall to the ground? Harry Emerson Fosdick, mid-twentieth century writer and clergyman, said, "Hating people is like burning down your own house to get rid of a rat."

> *Resentment, one of the core elements of unforgive-ness, is like carrying around a red-hot rock with the intention of someday throwing it back at the one who hurt you. It tires us and burns us. Who wouldn't want simply to let the rock fall to the ground?*

Third, "You will be healthier if you forgive than if you stew in your unforgiveness." I knew the research literature. There's a lot of evidence suggesting that hostility causes cardiovascular difficulties. Also, chronic stress is related to poor immune system functioning. However, research on forgiveness is so new, we cannot yet make definitive statements about its effects, although I believe forgiveness *probably* reduces health risk.

"Forgiveness can help reconcile damaged relationships and make people healthier," some argue. Forgiveness can indeed give me more joy with a partner, friend, or coworker than staying bitter. Forgiveness is a conduit through which love can flow between partners. That is common sense. Yet again, research on forgiveness in relationships is only in the early stages, and so we don't want to claim the matter is fact. Besides, I didn't have a relationship with the youth who killed my mother.

I knew the arguments in both the do-forgive and don't-forgive stories. As I paced the bedroom, though, I didn't know which story to listen to.

Who Won the Debate?

Lots of thoughts flashed through my mind that night. I didn't evaluate them like Mr. Spock or Data. I considered point and counterpoint, but my thoughts were jumbled. On the whole, I thought that I *ought* to forgive. Even the mental picture of a blood-soaked carpet couldn't dislodge that conviction.

Honestly, though, I did not *want* to forgive. Even if I came around to wanting to forgive, I did not know if I *could* forgive.

In the end, however, it was not relentless reasons or even Christian conviction that tipped the scales against ugly unforgiveness. I merely became weary of struggling against hatred. My emotions drove me to try to forgive.

> *In the end, however, it was not relentless reasons or even Christian conviction that tipped the scales against ugly unforgiveness. I merely became weary of struggling against hatred. My emotions drove me to try to forgive.*

At the emotional crest of that difficult, dark night, I wanted relief from my anger. I needed a rock that would steady my reeling views of the world and myself. I wanted to forgive if it would help me deal with my pain, anger, hurt, and sadness. *If only I could forgive,* I thought, *I could have peace in my heart.* I wanted a powerful emotional chemical that could neutralize the acid of hate and rage that gnawed at me.

Forgiveness: Is It for Giving or for Getting?

Even as I thought of being free of my struggles, though, I recalled our research programs for helping people forgive. Between 1985 and 1995, my colleagues and I—as both a therapist and a scientist who had studied more than 1,000 couples or individuals—helped people who wanted to forgive but had tried and failed—often for years. In three separate studies, we had compared two conditions, which we called a self-benefit condition and an empathy-based condition.

In the self-benefit condition, we asked people to forgive so that they could get personal benefits. We detailed the likely health consequences of chronic unforgiveness. We suggested the positive health consequences of forgiving. We told them, "Forgive. You'll be free. You'll be able to move on with your life." We showed people how to use imagery, let go of anger, release resentment, cut the chains that bound them to the person who hurt or offended them. We helped them relax. We taught them how to lower the stress of unforgiveness. In short, we appealed to the same motives and emotions that cried within me: *Forgive so you'll feel better.*

I remembered a person I'll call Marci. Marci wanted the freedom of forgiveness. She was forty-five years old but felt at least sixty. She knew that forgiveness was the right thing for her to do. But knowing and doing are different.

Her difficulties began with a little thing. Her husband's car was rear-ended by a city bus. The car wasn't even that damaged, but Bruce, her husband, continued to have pain in his neck. Finally, his physician suggested that surgery might repair the damaged disks between the vertebrae. During the operation, something went terribly wrong, and the surgeon cut the spinal cord. Bruce had not been able to walk for eleven years.

Bruce's injury put an enormous burden on Marci and their two children. Every day Marci cursed the bus driver who hadn't paid attention, the physician who had recommended neck surgery, and the surgeon who had botched it.

Now Marci was getting sick. She felt run-down from the unremitting demands of caring for Bruce and rearing two adolescents.

Her stomach was always upset. Her mother, herself a crotchety sixty-five-year-old, called Marci "old before your time." Marci knew her mother was right. Bitterness was poisoning every day and had stripped Marci's life of happiness. But she didn't seem to be able to do anything about it. She wanted to forgive the targets of her hatred because she wanted to feel better. Forgiveness was the royal road to health, she thought. Our self-benefit intervention would have been tailor-made for Marci.

Forgiving Is for Giving

In the empathy-based condition, we asked people to forgive because the perpetrator needs forgiveness: "You are the only one who can give him [or her] what he [or she] needs: forgiveness." We appealed to people's altruistic motives to give a gift of forgiveness to a needy person rather than to get relief from unforgiveness.

Frankly, this is a difficult sell. When people are angry, resentful, and bitter toward a person, the last thing they want to do is something nice for that person. Yet most people, if they hang with us, change their heart. They come to see that anger, resentment, hostility, rage, and hatred are motives to destroy. They know that while destroying a hated object can feel good for a while, lasting satisfaction comes more often with creating.

Before Kirby and I married, I lived alone in Boston. I was in love with her but very lonely. I would sit in Storrow Park along the Charles River and watch happy lovers laugh and talk with each other. I began to write poetry. That urge to fill the hole of sorrow was born of a longing for something more in my life than I was experiencing. I could have raged against fate, circumstances, or a hateful God that kept Kirby and me apart. Instead I wrote poetry. I created something that had not existed before—poems that expressed my love and passion. I was proud of my creations.

I was pleased to show them to Kirby. I had put part of me into those poems.

An amazing change took place. I put a piece of myself into creation, yet I was not diminished. In fact, I somehow felt I was more than what I had been. By creating, I used a piece of my heart to bless someone else. Yet my heart grew larger within me. I didn't write poetry to grow a larger heart. I wrote to share a piece of my heart to bless the one I cared about. But the surprise was, I grew in the process.

In our empathy-based groups, we appealed to people's altruistic motives. "Empathize with the one who hurt you until you can identify with his or her humanity," we would say. "Then consider whether you have ever hurt people. We are connected to all people. We all do despicable acts at times. So in that way you are similar to the one who hurt you. Now consider whether you would like to do something good for the one who hurt you. You can give a gift that only you can give: forgiveness for that injury to you."

THE COMPARISON

When we compared the self-benefit and empathy-based groups, we found consistent results. One study involved brief one-hour programs. The other involved eight-hour programs. People who forgave in the self-benefit group achieved more forgiveness right away than did those who forgave in the empathy-based group. Longer treatment didn't help those who forgave for their own benefit. One hour or eight hours—forgiveness for one's own benefit was modest. For those who forgave for the other person's benefit, one hour produced a little forgiveness. Eight hours produced a lot of forgiveness—over five times as much forgiveness as one hour, and three times as much as the self-benefit condition.

Furthermore, when we checked in with people six weeks later, the level of forgiveness in the self-benefit group had dropped to half as much as had been granted at the end of treatment. In the empathy-based group, the level of forgiveness stayed high even after the intervention was complete.

We've all heard "Forgive and forget," but forgiving seems to be for *giving,* not for *getting.* When we forgive, we get an immediate sense of personal peace. If we practice forgiving over a lifetime, chances are that we will be healthier in the long run. Our immune systems might function better. We might be at less risk for cardio-vascular disease. If we forgive, we can also give a gift of peace to the person who hurt us, and we might repair the relationship and therefore have more harmonious social support systems. If we forgive, our entire community might focus less on revenge, avoidance, unforgiveness, and past problems and move on to future possibilities. Away from hurt and on to healing.

Forgiveness does benefit us. But if we forgive mainly to get, we get just a trickle of all those benefits. If we give a gift of forgiveness to a needy perpetrator, though, we receive freedom, peace, and perhaps health and relational repair. Forgiveness gushes like water from a fire hose. It washes us clean. It frees us.

> *Forgiveness does benefit us. But if we forgive mainly to get, we get just a trickle of all those benefits. If we give a gift of forgiveness to a needy perpetrator, though, we receive freedom, peace, and perhaps health and relational repair. Forgiveness gushes like water from a fire hose. It washes us clean. It frees us.*

In a way, forgiveness is like air. If we close our fist, trying to grasp air, it squeezes through our clutching fingers, but if we simply breathe deeply and exhale, then we can both get the oxygen and warm those by whom our breath passes. In the same way, if we try to clutch the benefits of forgiveness for ourselves by forgiving because we want better health, because we want more peace, we seem to in some way contaminate the full power of those benefits. We get a discounted version of the benefits. But if we try to bless others by forgiving, then paradoxically we are flooded with blessings ourselves. Forgiving is for giving, not for getting.

How My Story and Yours Might Meet

I knew all these things about forgiveness when I found that Mama had been murdered. That event rocked me. I questioned what I knew and what I believed. I wrestled with my emotions. Since the murder, I have changed and grown through my struggles, and I will tell you about some of those struggles as we move through each chapter of the book.

Now, more than five years later, I want to share with you my journeys through personal experience and scientific study—through the heart and science of forgiving. I will show you how to forgive those events and people you might have tried to forgive but could not. I will show you how to pursue reconciliation if you are in relationships with damaged trust. I will show you how to practice a more forgiving lifestyle.

If I am successful with this book, you will look at forgiveness, reconciliation, and how to understand and experience them differently than when you picked up the book. I hope to gently challenge the story of self-focus that we seem to have adopted in our culture to explain the miracle of forgiveness. I hope to help you look at and practice forgiveness differently from now on.

From the Gray of Dorothy's Kansas to the Color of Oz

I experienced such a change in perception one day. It was a July summer in Richmond, Virginia, and the temperature was about 104 degrees Fahrenheit. A brief thundershower had just ended, and the steam was literally rising from the pavement in waves that distorted vision. Traffic had become snarled in one lane, perhaps because of a fender-bender down the street somewhere, and the second lane was barely moving.

As I walked down the street, a drama unfolded before my eyes. I saw a man driving in the lane that was barely moving almost go crazy. He pounded on his horn furiously, slamming his hand onto the steering wheel again and again. The car in front of him had stopped, and the driver had left the car in the middle of the lane of traffic noxiously belching exhaust fumes. The man walked toward one of the psychology buildings at Virginia Commonwealth University. The steam coming from the pavement seemed nothing compared to the steam that almost seemed to be shooting from the ears of the irate driver. The driver jerked open his door, fought his way out of his vehicle, kicked the door shut, and stalked toward the car in front of him. I thought I was going to see road rage. "Driver throws automobile two city blocks," the news anchor might say. "Details at eleven."

Just as the irate driver reached the abandoned car, the door to the psychology building opened and the driver of the abandoned car struggled out, holding a child in his arms. The child's legs were withered, and she had braces on both feet. The driver lurched toward the car as fast as he could, carrying his crippled burden.

When the irate driver heard the steps approaching from behind, he whirled around with a scowl and almost took a step toward the driver who was carrying the child. But no sooner had the irate driver moved than he realized what was happening. His eyes widened. The squint softened. The jaw muscles slackened. He stepped back and, like a doorman at the Ritz-Carlton, opened the car door with a flourish for the man to place the child inside the vehicle. I could almost hear his heels click. This irate driver experienced a change in his view of the situation that made all of his old ideas irrelevant and set him toward a path of compassion because of his empathy for the man who was carrying the child.

I believe that if you follow the reasoning in this book, you will see forgiveness differently than you might have before. I also hope that you will think of forgiveness as a way to give to others something they need. You might not believe it could happen now, but I hope that by the end of this book you might even wish well to those who have offended and hurt you.

Long-Term Rewards of Developing a Forgiving Character

I was alarmed at the hatred, anger, and bitterness that had revealed itself in my own life so quickly. The violence of attack against my mother had stripped away some of my tenaciously held self-delusion that kept me believing that I was habitually kind, loving, and forgiving. Confronting my own unforgiveness was a powerful shock.

As a Christian, I long to live a virtuous life. Yet I know enough of my dark side to know that my motivations are probably always tainted. Looking back, I now see how, even as I was consumed by unforgiveness, fantasies of revenge, resentments at life and society, and the beginnings of bitterness, a small voice whispered within me to at least *consider* a forgiving response to the murder. We often underestimate the power of that desire for a virtuous character. Yet it pulls us along if we but listen.

Pursuing forgiveness—not just as an act, not just as a response to a particular troublesome person, but as a character trait—is a goal for many people. We follow this path toward virtue, on which there are obstacles, ruts, and side trails that lead us off into the bushes, landmarks that allow us to evaluate our progress, giants that block our way, passing lanes that speed our progress in relationships, and even bridges that must be crossed.

The way of forgiveness is hard. Forgiveness isn't for wimps and wusses. In many ways, the destructive power of unforgiveness is much easier than the tough, steely pull of forgiveness. Still, if we follow forgiveness, we will become more loving.

> *The way of forgiveness is hard. Forgiveness isn't for wimps and wusses. In many ways, the destructive power of unforgiveness is much easier than the tough, steely pull of forgiveness.*

In this book, I tell my story, bit by bit in each chapter, as a way to help you forgive those with whom you are having difficulty. In Part 1, I consider how we forgive—whether we are in a continuing relationship with another or whether the person is estranged, has moved, or is dead. Then in Part 2, I describe how to reconcile with a person with whom you want to or must continue to interact.

Both Christianity and modern culture have much to say about forgiving. I have learned from both. I have been greatly privileged to serve as executive director for A Campaign for Forgiveness Research by the Templeton Foundation. After codirecting a scien-

tific competition to award $3 million to the best research propos-
als from more than two hundred applicants, which included some
of the top research laboratories in the world, I was asked to direct
the Campaign to raise additional support to fund even more research on forgiveness. Between late 1998 and early 2001, we
raised an additional $3.4 million to support these world-class re-
searchers. Associating with these internationally renowned scientists and monitoring their research have taught me much about
all aspects of forgiveness—from the struggles of individuals, couples, and families to conflict in cultures to parallel processes in
chimpanzees.

In this book, I concentrate on the aspects of how to forgive
that are informed more by science than by religion, the humanities, or our personal experiences. I believe that all three voices mix
together in intricate harmony. So I try to blend some of the different voices into the song I sing to you about how we can more
deeply forgive.

Each step in the Pyramid Model to REACH Forgiveness is
easy to understand. Each practical exercise is easy to do, and hundreds of people have tried them. If you put these exercises into
practice, you can forgive events that have been unforgiven for
years. Yet don't be deceived. Forgiveness is as mysterious as love. I
have forgiven some horrendous offenses in hours and nursed
petty grudges for years.

I invite you to come with me as I describe some of my
experiences—personally, as a counselor, and as a researcher. If you
have been devastated by a gaping emotional wound or if you have
a nagging personal abrasion, let's consider our mutual experiences
in unforgiveness and forgiveness.

PART ONE

✱

HOW TO FORGIVE

CHAPTER I

Laying the
Foundation

*We talk a good forgiving line as long as somebody else
needs to do it, but few of us have the heart for it while we
are dangling from one end of a bond broken by somebody
else's cruelty.*

—LEWIS B. SMEDES

Unforgiveness is a jumble of emotions. Resentment, hostility,
hatred, bitterness, simmering anger, and low-level fear in-
terlace in the tapestry of unforgiveness.

Unforgiving emotions are not "hot" (i.e., immediate) reactions to a transgression. They are ignited by the spark of perceived
hurt or offense, fanned by the hot emotions of anger and fear,
damped to a slow burn by time, and scuffed into a stack of dangerous coals by rumination. Unforgiveness is emotion served
"cold" (i.e., delayed). But like dry ice, which can burn the fingers,
unforgiveness can still scorch the gut. Unforgiveness motivates
people to get rid of those unpleasant emotions.

Maybe the best way to understand unforgiveness is to look at a flow chart that illustrates the process of moving from the initial insult to resolution.[1] (See Figure 1.1.) In the first step, a transgression is perceived as a hurt or an offense. This hurt stimulates fear (of being hurt again) and anger. Important: Fear and anger, immediate responses, are not unforgiveness. Unforgiveness must ripen through rumination. Only after mentally replaying the transgression, the motives of the transgressor, or the consequences of the transgression do we become unforgiving. It takes time and reflection to arrive at this stage.

Rob was unforgiving. When I met him, he was wearing a shirt picturing a flaming city against a black background. The caption read Rage Against the Machine (the name of a rock band known for its angry protests against social injustices). Rob had recently been released from his drug rehabilitation program. Living on the street in the Northeast, he had paid for his drug habit by borrowing until his friends ran out, begging until his patience ran out, and bartering until the stolen goods ran out. With the approach of winter, he scraped up enough money for a bus ticket and headed south. Picked up for vagrancy and drug intoxication in Florida, he had served his time and then headed for a rehabilitation center. Rob was twenty years old.

Rob blamed a lot of people for his troubles. He blamed his father, who had kicked him out after Rob struck his mother during an argument that broke out when Rob came home high on drugs. Rob blamed his high school love, who had introduced him to the party scene. He blamed his college philosophy professor, who preached hedonism. Mostly, Rob blamed his "quote friends unquote," who took him in after his father had rejected him, bled him of everything he owned, then turned him out on the street.

Rob could name the transgressions against him with ease. He perceived each transgression mostly as a personal offense by "the

FIGURE I.I
Understanding Forgiveness*

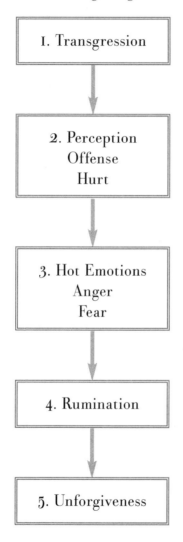

I. Transgression
2. Perception / Offense / Hurt
3. Hot Emotions / Anger / Fear
4. Rumination
5. Unforgiveness

* Reprinted from *Fordham Urban Law Journal* (2000), Worthington.

bastards." His dominant emotion was anger, with a subtheme of hurt and fear etching a whine into his complaints. Rob ruminated continually on his situation. He complained. He ranted. He mumbled about "the bastards" to himself and to anyone who would listen (and some who would not listen). Rob was a poster boy for unforgiveness.

Unforgiveness is defined as delayed emotions involving resentment, bitterness, residual anger, residual fear, hatred, hostility, and stress, which motivate people to reduce the unforgiveness. There are two important parts to this definition: Unforgiveness is an emotion, and unforgiveness motivates people to get rid of or avoid negative emotion. Let's consider each.

> *Unforgiveness is defined as delayed emotions involving resentment, bitterness, residual anger, residual fear, hatred, hostility, and stress, which motivate people to reduce the unforgiveness.*

Unforgiveness Is an Emotion

Rumination, the process of reflection on what's hurt us, changes the hot emotions of fear and anger into cold emotions of unforgiveness. The key to this model, and to my description of how you might forgive, is my understanding of *emotion* (Figure 1.2).

Emotions are not feelings. Feelings are the ways we label emotions in a part of the brain called the working memory. We say, "I feel angry," or "I feel loving." That feeling is our conscious mind's way of using a word to describe what is going on all over our body and is being communicated to the brain.

Emotions are *embodied* experiences. Antonio Damasio, per-

FIGURE 1.2
Understanding Emotion

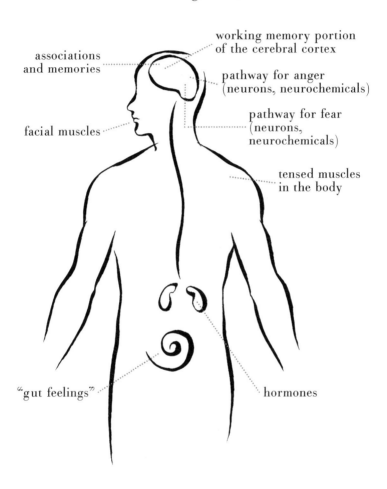

working memory portion
of the cerebral cortex

associations
and memories

pathway for anger
(neurons, neurochemicals)

pathway for fear
(neurons,
neurochemicals)

facial muscles

tensed muscles
in the body

"gut feelings"

hormones

haps the leading expert on emotion in the world, has studied them for years.

When we experience an emotion, each part of our body tells the brain precisely what emotion we are experiencing by sending either chemical messengers through the blood or chemical and electrical messengers through the nervous system. These messengers activate the memories of past emotions into the part of our brain called the association cortex, located in our prefrontal lobe. The pathways from these associations are fed into the working memory.

As the messengers travel through our nervous system, electric currents rush along neurons through brain structures such as the amygdala and hippocampus saying, "This path means 'I'm afraid,' " or "This path means 'I am happy.' " Neurochemicals squirt into some portions of the brain when we are sad and other portions when we are angry, afraid, or happy. The patterns of neurochemical release tell our working memory about our emotions.

As the messengers travel through the bloodstream, they cause the release of hormones. One mixture tells the working memory we are angry. Another mixture tells the working memory we are afraid.

Our muscles get into the act. When we are angry, we clench our fists, hunch our shoulders, and grind our teeth. When we are afraid, we widen our eyes, draw backward, and inhale. When we are calm, our face relaxes or smiles. Those muscles also send messages to the working memory.

Even our gut sends unconscious messages to the working memory. Damasio has found that the gut shouts an alarm over a risky decision long before the brain can figure out the message consciously.[2]

Our working memory is a supercomputer that listens to the body and decodes its many chemical and electrical messages, coming up with a *feeling*. "I feel angry," we might say.

Because emotions are whole-body experiences, they often blend if they are relatively similar. For instance, anger, fear, and sadness are all perceived negatively, especially if they are experienced intensely. Joy, happiness, and satisfaction are also relatively similar and are perceived positively. Similar emotions can blend with each other, forming a secondary, more complex emotion. For instance, the negative emotions of resentment, bitterness, hatred, hostility, anger, fear, and stress blend into the feeling people label "unforgiveness."

However, when emotional states are very different, they don't blend. They compete. For instance, when our facial muscles are set in a grimace of anger, that grimace edges out a soft smile of happiness and peace or even a frown of distress. The patterns of hormones in the blood or neurochemicals in the brain also compete. Different emotions light up different pathways and structures in the brain.

For instance, try this experiment. Look in the mirror and make a face that might show you are angry. Then look afraid. Now try to look angry and afraid at the same time. With effort, you can make the two negative emotions blend on your face.

Now do this. Look angry. Then look happy. Try to put them together. Your face simply will not cooperate. The brain will get only one signal at a time.

Perhaps you could confuse your brain by switching rapidly from anger to happiness, but with naturally occurring emotions, fooling the brain would be no easy task. Thought processes can change quickly, but hormones dumped into the blood or neurotransmitters squirted into the brain respond more slowly. That is why we can be in a sad mood and laugh at a joke but return immediately to feeling sad.

Unforgiveness Motivates Us to Get Rid of Negative Emotion

Unforgiveness is a hot potato. People try to pass it on as soon as they can. All negative emotions are unpleasant, especially when they are intense. We usually like to get rid of those feelings quickly. Sometimes our goal is simply to get rid of the unpleasant feelings, other times it's to radically change from negative to positive emotions.

Perhaps one of the strongest examples of this can be seen in the case of parents needing to forgive their children. Njeri was an educator and often spoke to PTAs and groups of parents on parenting. She was also the single parent of Rashid. Rashid obviously had a mind of his own. He was flunking sixth grade and often got in trouble with his teachers. One month earlier, he had been caught breaking windows at the school at night. Njeri knew that her reputation as an educator and trainer of parents was irreparably damaged by Rashid's willfulness.

She felt like a failure at parenting. She had tried the hard line. She had taken away Rashid's privileges, restricted television, and monitored his friends. Still he acted out. She knew he now would have to face the juvenile authorities, and it wasn't just he who was on trial. Her parenting was going to be judged as well.

Over the month, Njeri's resentment had grown. She sometimes thought, *I hate that boy.* She was aware that her negativity was pushing him further into deviance. If things were going to turn around, she would have to do something drastic.

Njeri instinctively knew that she needed new emotions. She didn't want merely to reduce her anger toward Rashid. She wanted to feel more compassion and love for him, not just less rage. She needed to forgive him so that they could start afresh and rebuild their mutual love. Eventually, she was able to forgive Rashid and develop a more positive attitude. Rashid did not respond immediately, but he finally changed his group of friends and moved away from the troubled path he had been following.

People Reduce Unforgiveness in Many Ways

Most people think of forgiveness as "the way you reduce unforgiveness." But there are many ways people reduce unforgiveness that have nothing to do with forgiveness.

To take a trivial example, I could reduce my unforgiveness through successful revenge. Suppose I was walking out of my office holding my ever-present cup of coffee in my forever-coffee-cup-molded right hand. A mysterious stranger bumps into me, spilling coffee on my favorite 1970s pink-with-polka-dots power tie. After an initial burst of anger, I seethe with the lust for revenge. Donning my genuine Arnold Schwarzenegger *Terminator* trench coat, complete with an arsenal of weaponry that would make any National Rifle Association member envious, I track down the mysterious stranger and blow him away. My unforgiveness would have been reduced, perhaps eliminated, by successful revenge. Of course, I would never recommend revenge. It's like overeating. It might feel good while you're doing it, but it will give you a sour stomach in the morning and health problems if it becomes habitual.

We can use many other methods to reduce unforgiveness. Seeing justice done can reduce unforgiveness. In the movie made from Sister Helen Prejean's book *Dead Man Walking,* the murderer is about to be put to death by lethal injection. He faces the parents of the two youths he killed. To one father he says, "I hope that seeing

my death will give you peace." He instinctively knew that seeing justice done would reduce the grieving father's unforgiveness,
but not necessarily lead to forgiveness.

People can also reduce unforgiveness by telling a different
story about the transgression or transgressor. "He was just under
stress" might excuse the transgression. "I was rude to her, so I deserved what she said" might justify it. Excusing or justifying a
slight will reduce the storyteller's unforgiveness.

People can reduce unforgiveness by forbearing or simply accepting a transgression. "What's done is done," a person might
say. "I'm just going to accept it and move on with my life."

Sometimes our best course of reducing unforgiveness is seeking justice. At other times, we tell a different story or simply accept the injustice. Sometimes, though, we want to do more than
simply reduce the negative emotions. We want to replace them
with more positive emotions. That is where forgiveness enters the
picture.

FORGIVENESS IS EMOTIONAL REPLACEMENT

Forgiveness is defined as *the emotional replacement of (1) hot
emotions of anger or fear that follow a perceived hurt or offense,
or (2) unforgiveness that follows ruminating about the transgression,
by substituting positive emotions such as unselfish love, empathy,
compassion, or even romantic love.* If these positive emotions are
strong enough and last long enough, they "contaminate" the
unforgiveness so that it can never be experienced in the same way
again. Emotional "replacement" has occurred. We experience
forgiveness.

*Forgiveness is defined as the emotional replacement
of (1) hot emotions of anger or fear that follow a per-*

*ceived hurt or offense, or (2) unforgiveness that follows
ruminating about the transgression, by substituting positive emotions such as unselfish love, empathy, compassion,
or even romantic love.*

It is important to understand what I mean by emotional replacement. Our hurtful memories are not really wiped out. We almost never really forget serious hurts or offenses. We remember
them differently after we forgive. Hate, bitterness, and resentment
are replaced with positive thoughts and feelings. The memory of
the hurt remains, but it is associated with different emotions.
Amity is substituted for enmity.

There are two ways to eliminate unforgiveness. First, you
could chip away at it by replacing a little unforgiveness with a
little forgiveness over hundreds of experiences. Second, you could
whack unforgiveness with a giant dose of empathy, sympathy,
compassion, or love and simply overwhelm it. (One woman I
know reponds to perceived slights by sending the transgressor a
"love bomb," which blows her bad feelings to bits—a vivid way of
describing how positive emotion can disarm hurt feelings.)

Forgiving emotions motivate us to attempt conciliation or reconciliation if—and sometimes it is a big if—it is safe, prudent,
and possible to reconcile. *Reconciliation is reestablishing trust in a
relationship after trust has been violated.*

*Reconciliation is reestablishing trust in a relation-
ship after trust has been violated.*

Note that forgiveness does not erase a transgression. It does
not change the nature of the transgression to somehow turn a
wrong into a right. When we forgive, we change the emotional

attachments to the transgression. That reduces negative emotions and increases positive emotions.

How Emotional Replacement Works

I have stated briefly how emotional replacement works. Let me be more explicit. Emotional replacement is possible because emotions are *embodied experiences* involving those gut feelings, rushes of hormones, muscle contractions, facial expressions, brain pathways, neurotransmitter patterns, memories, and associations that I described earlier. Our working memory sorts out the messages from our body.

Basically, we are simple-minded. When we think about a transgression, our body sends messages to the working memory. Our brain detects our hormones. Are those hormones the ones associated with resentment, bitterness, hostility, and hatred? Or are they compatible with empathy, sympathy, compassion, and love? Are our muscle contractions, facial expressions, and other physical indications more like unforgiveness or forgiveness? The working memory struggles for, and arrives at, a label for our *feelings*. If all the signs translate into negative emotions, we think, *Ah, I must be unforgiving,* even if we don't consciously use that term.

Here's how replacement occurs. If we can think of or picture the transgression again, but this time while experiencing strong forgiving emotions, the positive overpowers the negative. The forgiving emotions attach to the memory. We conclude, "I forgive the one who hurt me." The attached forgiveness won't let you experience unforgiveness in the same way again—unless you have another negative experience or allow yourself to ruminate about the old transgression.

Here's Looking at You, Kid

A good example comes from the classic movie *Casablanca*. Rick (Humphrey Bogart) and Ilsa (Ingrid Bergman) were once lovers. Then Ilsa found out that her husband, Victor Laszlo, whom she thought was dead, was still alive. Ilsa loved Rick, not Victor, but she felt duty-bound to return to Victor. So she left Rick at the airport. Jilted. Rejected.

Rick nursed his grudge. Later Ilsa and Victor walked into Rick's club in Casablanca hoping to escape the Nazis. Rick held the only two letters of transit out of Casablanca. His unforgiveness was fierce. He lusted for revenge.

However, his romantic love for Ilsa was rekindled. It eventually subdued his unforgiveness, and in the end, he let Ilsa and Victor escape into the fog with the two letters while he stayed in Casablanca to fight the Nazis. We see step by step how Rick's emotional replacement evolves. And it's the stuff of great cinema.

Forgiveness occurs by emotional replacement of the emotions of unforgiveness—either by chipping away at them or by replacing them all at once in a corrective emotional experience. That is the foundation on which the structure of how to forgive will be erected.

You've Got Male (and Female)

Because the idea of emotional replacement is so important, let me give you another brief example of how forgiving replaces unforgiveness. I will use romantic love as the positive emotion because in real-life romantic relationships and marriages, reexperiencing romantic love is often the key to defeating unforgiveness.

The movie *You've Got Mail* played forgiveness in an electronic key. Tom Hanks portrayed Joe Fox, owner of a chain of giant bookstores. Meg Ryan's character was the owner of a small family-run bookstore. Hanks drove Ryan out of business. "It's nothing personal," he said. But to Ryan, it was nothing but personal. She felt offended, wronged, and hurt. She became unforgiving.

Meanwhile Ryan and Hanks developed a relationship via e-mail—corresponding with each other using pseudonyms. Neither knew the name behind the pseudonym. Hanks discovered Ryan's true identity first, but continued to hide his own.

Their love grew as they got to know each other both via e-mail (still using pseudonyms) and through personal interaction (in which Hanks tried to win over an unsuspecting Ryan). But Ryan's unforgiveness was still stronger than her love. In the climactic scene, she discovered that Hanks was the same person she had come to know and love through e-mail. That extra amount of affection melted her heart. "I wanted it to be you," she said.

It took a long time, but when the feelings of love overpowered the feelings of unforgiveness, Meg Ryan forgave and things changed dramatically. Forgiveness was like flipping a light switch from off to on. Her heart lit up.

Forgiveness is kicking down the Berlin Wall, chipping away at it hammer blow by hammer blow or blowing it suddenly apart. When the wall is breached, people can run through the holes into freedom.

FORGIVENESS IS NOT JUST . . .

I have made the case that forgiveness is an emotional experience. There are many other ways people understand it. Some people think of forgiveness as merely an act of the will. They think, *I must grit my teeth and forgive because it is the right thing to do. If I can will myself to forgive, then forgiving thoughts and forgiving emo-*

tions and behaviors will follow naturally. I agree that sometimes forgiving involves effort and will. They empower us to forgive, but they are not forgiveness.

Still other people believe that forgiveness is a mental activity. They think that changing one's view of the situation, thinking differently about the person, or coming to understand the meaning of the situation differently will result in different emotions and different behaviors. True, forgiveness often is instigated when we break out of old thought ruts. However, sometimes we forgive and only later does a new understanding occur.

Other people believe that forgiveness is an action. They believe that if we act forgiving toward a person, our changed behavior will result in changed thoughts and emotions. Sometimes changing my behavior can result in experiencing forgiveness. Sometimes my soft action can make it easier to forgive.

I argue—I hope convincingly—that you cannot experience true forgiveness until you change your emotions. If people change their will, thought, or actions to be more forgiving, it will not bring about forgiveness until their emotions change.

The Pyramid Model to REACH Forgiveness is rooted in replacing negative emotions associated with anger, fear, and unforgiveness with positive emotions associated with empathy (and perhaps sympathy, love, compassion, or even romantic love). It helps people REACH forgiveness in five steps.

Overview of the Pyramid Model to REACH Forgiveness

First, to get a bird's-eye view, walk with me up the pyramid (Figure 1.3). The steps spell out the acrostic REACH.

Recall the hurt (R). When we are hurt, we often try to protect ourselves by denying our hurt. To heal, we must recall the hurt as objectively as possible. Don't rail against the person who hurt you, expend fruitless effort in finger wagging, waste time wishing for an apology that will never be offered, or dwell on your victimization. Instead, simply admit that a wrong was done to you.

Empathize (E). Empathy is seeing things from another person's point of view. To forgive, try to feel the transgressor's feelings.

FIGURE 1.3
The Pyramid Model to REACH Forgiveness

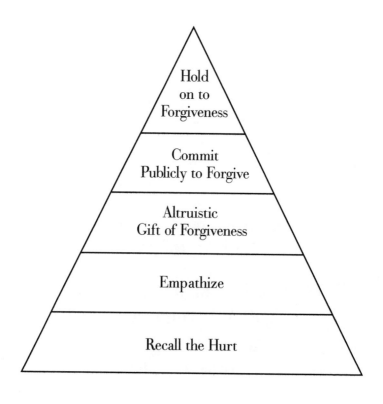

Even though it is difficult, try to identify with the pressures that made the person hurt you. Empathy puts a human face on suffering. How would he or she explain the harmful acts?

Offer the altruistic gift of forgiveness (A). Have you ever harmed or offended a friend, parent, or partner who later forgave you? Think about your guilt. Then consider the way you felt when you were forgiven. When you think long and hard about this, you might be willing to be selfless and give the gift of forgiveness to those who have hurt you.

Commit publicly to forgive (C). If you make your forgiveness public, you are less likely to doubt it later. Tell a friend, partner, or counselor that you have forgiven the person who hurt you.

Hold on to forgiveness (H). When you doubt whether you have forgiven, there are many ways to stop forgiveness from sliding back into anger, hurt, or thoughts of vengeance.

Putting the Pyramid Model into Practice

Knowing that you must take five steps to forgive is not the same as knowing how to take those steps. Sometimes we feel like Lilliputians trying to match Gulliver's giant strides. Forgiving seems impossible. However, in my research over the years, my colleagues and I have been able to help people take those giant steps by having them approach forgiveness in a measured, gradual way.

> *Forgiving seems impossible. However, in my research over the years, my colleagues and I have been able to help people take those giant steps by having them approach forgiveness in a measured, gradual way.*

You will forgive best if you identify specific people whom you might wish to forgive. Then you must practice trying to forgive each one. Apply the five steps to one person at a time. Think through your life and identify some people you want to forgive.

PEOPLE WHO MIGHT NEED YOUR FORGIVENESS

Transgressions can occur in almost any setting, but some settings seem to invite transgressions. See whether you can find people you need to forgive in these settings.

Romantic relationships put our egos on the line. We leave ourselves open to betrayal when we invest our love in another fallible human. Failed dating relationships, terminated cohabitation, and divorces provide much fuel for the fires of unforgiveness. Is there a romantic partner you want to forgive? Note some specific transgressions.

Families of origin influence us. Disappointments, hurts, misunderstandings, and simple cruelty may show up in both parents and children. Siblings often compete and quarrel. Children smolder over the long-ago hurts inflicted by parents. Families divide over contested wills. The family is a crucible for pounding out differences and a natural laboratory in which both forgiveness and reconciliation can be practiced. Are there incidents from your family history that still rankle? Write some notes.

In the *workplace,* time is spent in ego-involving tasks. Promotions, wages, and salaries can be used to prove you worthy or unworthy. Interactions with bosses or subordinates can value or devalue you. Scarce resources and power differentials set the stage for hurt feelings. Have you been transgressed against in the workplace?

Health care settings provide opportunities to forgive. The Institute of Medicine estimates that between 44,000 and 98,000 *medical errors* are made each year that lead to the death of a patient. Less fatal mishaps are even more common. Have you or has a loved one been a victim of a medical error? Has an arrogant physician, nurse, or health administrator demeaned you?

Perhaps you have run up against the *justice system.* Crimes against property and people usually result in drawn-out litigation. They usually end in plea bargains or settlements. Wronged parties' hard feelings often persist for years. Wrongdoers feel unfairly judged. Litigants do not believe they received a fair deal in property disputes. Arguments can be heated and hurtful. Every viewer of Judge Judy or Judge Wapner knows that. Have you experienced shortcomings of the justice system?

At the *end of life,* people try to make sense of their lives. They hate to leave the world with grudges. Forgiveness is a way to bring peace to their spirit. Reconciliation can bring peace to their relationships. Are you nearing the end of life? Whom do you want to forgive?

As the world becomes globally connected, we recognize how much our own context affects our understanding of others. In high school, the jocks don't hang out with the grunge crowd or the preps. Heavy metal clashes with hip-hop. The roots of *ethnic and class conflict* are often sewn in the wardrobe of in-groups and out-groups. Adult political groups play for higher stakes, such as taxes, political influence, or even ethnic cleansing. Unforgiveness can run wild in ethnic conflict. Failed forgiveness can flow like blood. Have you been hurt, offended, or discriminated against for your ethnicity, religion, age, sexual orientation, or gender? Who did it?

THREE QUESTIONS

You have considered several areas in which you might harbor unforgiveness. Perhaps you have recalled several specific incidents that you want to try to forgive. For each incident, ask yourself these questions. First, *how serious is the transgression?* Small transgressions annoy us. Large ones can turn our world upside down. Put off trying to forgive the ones that upset the world until you have gained confidence with smaller hurts. *How raw is the wound?* Don't choose to heal a wound while the blood is still wet. *Is the person you want to forgive absent from or present in your life?* In an ongoing relationship, the offending person will react to what you do. He or she can deliberately or accidentally hurt you again, which can compound the unforgiveness. Part 1 of the book will guide you in forgiving absent people. In Part 2, we will consider how to talk about transgressions and perhaps reconcile.

Think of at least four particular people whom you might practice forgiving as you read this book. For example, choose an absent person who inflicted only a few small hurts and whom you have already largely forgiven. That might be a schoolteacher who once said something to embarrass you. Perhaps you resented his or her remark for a while but have since forgiven most of the hurt. Only a thimbleful of unforgiveness remains.

Next, choose a second absent person who inflicted more severe wounds. Perhaps you have not yet forgiven that person.

At the other end of the spectrum, choose two people who are still present in your life—one who did few harms, one who did more harms. Maybe your best friend made a careless remark that insulted you and you still feel a bit miffed. On the other end of the spectrum, perhaps you might choose a parent who was particularly abusive to you when you were growing up and with whom you are still in close contact.

You will have the most success if you think of a specific incident in each case in which this person offended you. Write a short summary of each event now.

Remember, you cannot forgive in the abstract. Forgiveness occurs when you work through *specific events with specific people.* Reading a book about forgiveness will help you forgive a little, but not nearly as much as if you practice on the stories of hurt, betrayal, and anger you tell yourself.

We now have a bird's-eye view of the five steps to climb the Pyramid Model to REACH Forgiveness. In the next chapters, let's swoop in and take an up-close and personal look at each step.

CHAPTER 2

R: Recall the Hurt

Truth is the story of compost in which beauty may sometimes germinate.

—CHRISTOPHER MORLEY

Transgressions wound us. There are many varieties of wounds, from the five-cent variety to the five-hundred-dollar kind.

NICKEL WOUNDS

A nickel wound was inflicted on me as a struggling graduate student at the University of Missouri, Columbia. My wife, Kirby, and I moved into our first house, a two-bedroom crackerbox that had enough room in the master bedroom for a bed and a chest of drawers. If we got out of bed at the same time, we would bump into each other.

The summer that we bought the house, I planted a garden. I spaded twenty-five hundred square feet of hard ground by hand. Rototillers, I thought, were for the weak. The fact that the outdoor work kept me from studying was irrelevant.

When the spading was complete, I planted peas, perfect for an early-spring harvest. Soon the tender young shoots rose six inches

44

out of the ground. I admired the six fifty-foot rows of young pea plants. I was the Jolly Green Giant planting in magic soil.

The next morning I strolled down to the "lower forty." One and a half rows had been leveled. *A rabbit,* I thought grimly. Rage bubbled up inside of me. I concocted a plan.

Before sunrise the next morning, I armed myself with the only weapon I owned, a hammer. In my lawn chair, I assumed sentry duty. I sat in Mr. McGregor's garden in ambush for Peter Rabbit.

As dawn neared, motion caught my eye. A rabbit hopped purposefully past the house, underneath the apple tree, and across the ditch that separated the house from the garden.

As the rabbit approached, I flung the hammer at it. Of course, I missed. (I'm sorry if I have disillusioned you. I was avenging those helpless slaughtered peas.) The rabbit seemed unalarmed. It languidly took four hops back toward the house. I retrieved my hammer and flung it again. Not even close. This time the rabbit hopped perhaps eight hops away. It turned to squint at me with what seemed like a Clint Eastwood glare in its eyes. I could practically hear the theme song from *The Good, the Bad, and the Ugly.* I flung the hammer a third time. The rabbit scurried away. I followed it along the path it had come, across the road, through four other people's gardens, four blocks away. There I lost the trail. That rabbit had hopped through a half mile of other gardens to eat my peas. I hated that rabbit. Unforgiveness arose in my heart.

The next morning, wiser, I awaited the rabbit at the edge of the garden. This time, though, instead of being armed with a one-shot hammer, I carried a bag of rocks. (This is how the arms race in the Cold War got started.) As the rabbit approached, we faced off like gunslingers in a very bad Western. This time I had an AK-47 instead of a Smith & Wesson. I peppered the rabbit with the stones that I carried in my arms. After fifty tosses, I hit the rabbit in the side and stunned it. I closed in on the rabbit with raised stone. I saw its nose twitching, and its limpid eyes staring unblinking. Revenge screamed, "Finish it!"

Empathy whispered, "It's only doing what rabbits do." How important were those peas anyway? I dropped the rock and walked away. A nickel's worth of unforgiveness was not that hard to deal with. (Three days later, the peas were history.)

FIVE-DOLLAR WOUNDS

Five-dollar wounds are more severe. I had one of those in graduate school too. The professor of my behavioral psychology class seemed to be prejudiced against the counseling psychology students. He seemed to prefer the clinical psychology students. This being behavioral psychology, I of course immediately instituted systematic observation of the professor's behavior. I counted the number of times that he engaged in looking and speaking behavior with counseling psychologists as opposed to clinical psychologists. (That's the way behaviorists talk.)

As I suspected, he favored clinical psychology students. Or, as I thought of it, he emitted reinforcement behavior on a different schedule for counseling and clinical students. Being a counseling psychology student, of course, I was not happy about this.

At the end of the course, he gave me a B. I was aghast. How could he possibly do this to *me*? So I got even. For probably five years afterward, I nursed a five-dollar grudge against him for his unfair treatment. That showed him.

Another five-dollar wound arose when my wife and I were attempting to become pregnant with our fourth child. The first three children came almost exactly two years apart. I got overconfident about the pregnancy business. When it was time to attempt to conceive again, I was confident that that would occur quickly.

Month after month passed. No pregnancy. We tried all of the home remedies—taking Kirby's temperature, making love at the time of ovulation, elevating the hips after making love (hers, not mine). Nothing worked. We began to be concerned. Perhaps (gulp) I needed to have the potency of my semen tested.

I arrived for my appointment at the medical school clinic. In the center of the room sat a woman whom I affectionately think of, even today, as the Dragon Woman. She was armed with a clipboard. Her face was set into a perma-frown. Around the edge of the room were forty men, sitting on the edge of their chairs. They weren't anxious, just incredibly alert. I said quietly to the Dragon Woman, "I'm here to have my semen tested."

"What?" she yelled. I looked quickly around the room.

"I'm here to have my semen tested," I said a little louder.

"I can't hear you!" She shouted like the drill sergeant in a *Gomer Pyle* rerun.

"I'm here to have my semen tested!" I screamed. Forty pairs of eyes fixed upon me. I felt like crawling under the desk.

"Why didn't you say so?" she said. She reached under her desk. After fumbling around for a moment, she held up (for every eye to see) a flask. It was a *large* flask. A *very* large flask. "Fill 'er up," she said.

I swallowed heavily.

"Just kidding," she said. I took the flask, still looking at it apprehensively. I searched for privacy. I saw nothing available, so I looked inquiringly at her. "The bathroom is right behind you," she said, loudly enough for every ear to hear. Sure enough, the bathroom was right behind me. The public bathroom.

So I entered the very public bathroom. Being a keen observer, as psychologists often are, I immediately noticed that there were no doors on the stalls. Swell. Alone in the public bathroom, I got down to business. I wasn't alone long. Regular patrons of the bathroom walked in and out. They mumbled about what was going on in this public bathroom. The one with no doors on the stalls.

Finally, a miracle occurred. I pushed the flask underneath my coat and reported to the Dragon Woman. I sidled up to the table. I opened my coat so that she could see the flask, like someone selling Rolex watches for twenty-five bucks. I spoke out of the corner of my mouth. "Here's the semen sample."

She took the flask from me and held it up high (for everyone to see). She announced, seemingly at the top of her lungs, "That's not very much."

Now, that probably classifies as a five-dollar hurt. She defused the situation quickly by saying, "Naw, I'm only joking." (At least twenty men in the room let out audible sighs.) Even though I was embarrassed by her jokes, I knew her teasing was good-natured. It even made me laugh. I very quickly put the incident behind me.

Both my psychology professor and the Dragon Woman inflicted five-dollar wounds on me. One beaded up and rolled harmlessly off. The other soaked in and, as I worried it around my ego, it compounded its value until I made it worth at least twenty-five dollars of grudge.

FIFTY- AND FIVE-HUNDRED-DOLLAR WOUNDS

In contrast to the nickel and five-dollar wounds, a fifty-dollar wound leaves a lasting impression on people's lives. Let's return once again to the classic movie *Casablanca*. Rick was left standing in the rain at the train station. Rain splattered like tears on his Dear John letter. That was a fifty-dollar hurt. It changed Rick (and Ilsa) forever.

Five-hundred-dollar wounds irrevocably change people's lives.

My mother's murder was such a loss. The death of a loved one cannot be reversed. The pain of the grief will remain, regardless of what is done. One can always choose whether to compound the pain of the grief with a search for revenge, but the loss is permanent.

COUNTERFEIT-MONEY WOUNDS

I have heard people say that forgiveness is the way that we deal with "true offenses." With this reasoning, if my father beat me, that would be a true offense—one I might someday forgive. However, if I thought I'd overheard my father criticizing me but he really was not, then he did not truly offend. Forgiveness would not be appropriate.

I believe, however, that how we *perceive* an event determines whether we feel unforgiveness. Imagine a teacher lecturing to a class. Two women are talking. The teacher begins to feel that she cannot make her point because of the conversation between the women, so the teacher says, "You two, please stop talking."

One woman might think, *Who does that teacher think she is? She can't talk to me that way. I have a right to say what I want in this class. I paid my money, and I can talk if I wish.*

The other student might think, *I must be a terrible person for interrupting the class, taking everyone's time, and drawing attention away from the lesson. I am not worthy of the air that it takes to keep me alive. She has deeply wounded me by pointing this out to everyone.*

The teacher in this case was not offending either woman in an absolute sense. The teacher was within her rights to ask for silence from them. Yet one of the women perceived the teacher's fair and controlled reprimand as an offense, to which she responded with anger, and the other perceived the teacher's reprimand as an injury, to which she responded with pain and hurt. Both women might go home, ponder the event, and ruminate about it repeatedly until it generated a sense of unforgiveness.

Can they never forgive this teacher because this teacher truly did nothing wrong? Or did the anger and fear, which ripened into vengeful rumination, produce perceived transgressions that need forgiveness?

Whether one needs to forgive is not determined by objective circumstances. Who is to decide whether a "true" offense or hurt has occurred? If you experience unforgiving emotions, then you might need to forgive. Counterfeit-money hurts still wound.

How We Respond to Hurts and Offenses

Fear or Anger

Responses to hurt. When we have been hurt, our body and brain seek to avoid similar hurts. Emotions of fear are alarm bells that surround the memory. If similar threatening events, memories, or even thoughts of threat trip the alarm, then fear and anxiety quicken the breath, trigger adrenaline, and make us want to head for the hills to avoid hurt again.

Responses to offenses. When a person offends us, we get angry. Violations of fairness or justice are barriers to happiness. Anger makes us want to kick down the barriers.

Both are usually mixed, but one is stronger. An event that hurts one person might offend another. Our perception of an event and its meaning to us, not the event itself, stoke our emotional fires. Our perception of most events is not pure. I might perceive more hurt than offense (or vice versa), depending on my temperament and past experiences. I usually react with one emotion more than the other. Some people are easily hurt. They are the walking wounded—thin-skinned, tenderhearted, and fearful. They expect hurt and rejection. Others are volcanoes of offense and anger looking for a vent.

THE URGE TO RUN AWAY, FIGHT, OR KNUCKLE UNDER

Avoidance. Perceptions of hurt or offense and the accompanying emotions motivate us to avoid the transgressor. We might be hurt again. We might explode angrily. It's better to avoid the person, we conclude.

Retaliation or revenge. Retaliation is striking back with little forethought. Retaliation is a "hot" response. "Revenge is a dish best served cold," goes the saying. Revenge is plotted, planned, and executed in cold blood more than hot blood.

> *"Revenge is a dish best served cold," goes the saying. Revenge is plotted, planned, and executed in cold blood more than hot blood.*

Attack. Some hurts or offenses trigger more than mere retaliation or revenge. We might not be satisfied with a trickle of blood. We want to go for the jugular. We might attack because of hatred or self-preservation or because we consider someone to be a serious threat to our physical or psychological existence.

Withdraw and submit. Sometimes we are so intimidated by a transgressor that we dare not fight back, can't seek revenge, and cannot avoid. For survival, we knuckle under and submit.

SELF-PROTECTION

Denial. Mentally, we respond to transgressions by girding our loins and protecting ourselves. Our mind denies hurts or refuses to focus on painful memories.

Self-justification (by selective perception). The mind also can make us believe we are right, virtuous, and pure as the driven snow. We pay attention to and remember what is consistent with our story.

Both denial and self-justification are self-protective.

THE BODY TALKS BACK

Some people have their feelers up to detect hurts. They may have reactive nervous systems. Little things grate. Noises startle. Slights wound. Insults cause massive reactions. Because small hurts cause big reactions, such people are often filled with fears.

Others have personal radar detectors for being offended. They are hardwired for anger. The smallest slights are seen as insults. Insults are seen as egregious wrongs. These people are anger waiting for a place to happen.

Unforgiveness, though, is neither hurt nor fear, nor a mixture of the two. As I mentioned, unforgiveness is slow-cooked through vengeful rumination into resentment, hatred, hostility, anger, fear, stress, and bitterness. It is cacophony.

> *Unforgiveness is slow-cooked through vengeful rumination into resentment, hatred, hostility, anger, fear, stress, and bitterness.*

These jumbled emotions are likely to have health consequences. This is especially probable if you practice unforgiveness over a long time. The wages of chronic unforgiveness can be eventual illness—physical, moral, and spiritual.

In writing about women's health, psychotherapists Deborah Cox, Sally Stabb, and Karin Bruchner describe the case of Mary, a seventy-four-year-old great-grandmother.[1] Mary's life was focused on her ill health. That was not suprising given her thirteen surgeries. Mary's past involved severe abuse and punishment by her parents for expressing anger. She was once imprisoned in a garage for a day because she made a face when told to give her favorite toy to a neighbor. Mary's husband was frequently unfaithful. Mary kept gritting her teeth. She also got sicker and sicker. She had colitis, gallbladder problems, heart problems, upper respiratory troubles, migraine headaches, and hernias—to name a few of her problems. Mary's daughters, Janine and Sarah, both in family therapy, related that if they expressed their anger, Mary punished them. Unforgiveness sent a cascade rippling through Mary's body and her family, trickling pain down through the generations.

Unforgiveness builds a putrid lair scattered with bones, in which a giant dragon of self-absorption sits on its tin ruminations, thinking them to be solid gold. The dragon protects its hoard from invading counterimpulses of forgiveness and forbearance. Only love, empathy, compassion, and humility are strong and brave enough to enter the lair, slay the dragon, and thus alchemically transform the treasure into gold.

How Not to Recall the Hurt

For some of us whose unforgiving emotions lurk beneath a barely civil surface, allowing ourselves to recall our hurts and offenses can plunge us straight into rumination and thus bitter unforgiveness. To forgive, we must recall the hurt or offense, but we must do it differently than we usually do.

Perhaps we usually try to suppress feelings of unforgiveness. We deny that we feel hate. We think, *That hurt did not matter.* Instead of suppressing our feelings, we must come to grips with them. Instead of turning away from the pain and anger, we must face them.

Yet here's the catch. We must not glory in finger-pointing blame. Nor must we wallow in gut-wrenching self-pity. Remember Rick from *Casablanca.* Eventually he forgave Ilsa, but he made it difficult for himself by recalling Ilsa's rejection while drinking and feeling sorry for himself. Sam, the piano player, came in, and Rick ordered him to play "As Time Goes By"—Rick and Ilsa's song. "If she can stand it, so can I," Rick says without unclenching his jaw. Classic Bogart.

We must try not to think of the other person as a devil or as the personification of ill will toward us. When we have been hurt, it is easy to imagine that the person who hurt us did so because he or she despised us and organized his or her entire existence around ruining us. In the light of the midday sun, such a belief might seem like a paranoid delusion. When we are in the darkness of an angry and unforgiving mind, however, it can seem that the person has dedicated his or her life to destroying us.

As we think logically about our own lives, we know that we ourselves typically do not focus our lives around plotting someone's disaster, even if we hate the person. If we are honest with ourselves, we admit that we usually do not think much about our enemies. Any anger and malice toward them is only periodic. We need to give other people the same benefit of the doubt. Assume that their motives are not always negative and constantly directed toward destroying us.

When we recall the hurt, we should try to be as objective as we can be. We should try to remember accurately what the person did and what our responses were. Sometimes it helps to visualize what happened.

It is normal to remember the events that support our view of any situation. If I am unforgiving toward Mack, I will tend to remember the things that Mack did to hurt me. I'll forget what I did to provoke Mack. I'll remember my pain and unjust suffering. I'll forget my gossip about Mack and how it hurt his reputation. I'll remember his anger. I'll forget his contrition.

Sometimes when we remember a painful event, we can easily think of ourselves as innocent victims who were cruelly abused. While occasionally that is accurate, most of the time events that lead to unforgiveness have more than one side to them. (Of course, I usually look only at my side.)

To recall the hurt or offense, don't dwell on the negative. Try to be objective.

As you recall the hurt, take deep, slow breaths. Concentrate on fully exhaling. (If you empty your lungs, inhaling will take care of itself.) By exhaling deeply, you activate portions of the parasympathetic nervous system—the part of your autonomic nervous system that calms you. Calming breaths help you remember objectively.

Even if you breathe deeply, it might be difficult to recall the hurt, especially if the trauma was great. We do not like to reexperience negative feelings. Our mind protects us by shutting out negative memories. You can choose whether to recall painful events. The recall of trauma brings up strong feelings. If those feelings become unmanageable, stop thinking upsetting thoughts. Do something active. If you can't stop unwanted thoughts, seek the help of a psychologist, psychiatrist, counselor, or clergyperson.

However, just because it is painful to recall a trauma does not mean you should stuff the memory. If you consider the pain caused by unforgiveness, you might still want to face the pain of recall. Recalling the hurt or offense is the first step to healing.

Most hurts (painful as they are) are not traumas. As you selected events in your past on which to practice forgiving, I hope you did not choose the whoppers. To learn to use the Pyramid Model to REACH Forgiveness, choose the nickel or five-dollar wounds. When you have successfully forgiven them, then you are ready for the big money.

How I Recalled My Mother's Murder

I was still boiling mad as I paced the floor that first night in Knoxville, but I was convinced that I needed to at least try to forgive my mother's murderer. So I employed the Pyramid Model to REACH Forgiveness. It was, after all, research-tested. Despite helping hundreds of people forgive, I wasn't sure it would work for such a big wound. But it beat walking the floor.

At the heart of the method was recalling the offense and my hurt with empathy for the perpetrator. Empathy is a compassionate understanding of the perpetrator and the perpetrator's motives for doing the act of transgression, as I'll explain in much more detail in Chapter 3. I needed to think through the murder of my mother, as painful as that might be, in as much detail as I could. I knew I had to get inside the heads of those who might have committed that murder. I didn't *want* to do that. I *needed* to do it.

I imagined how two youths might feel as they prepared to rob a darkened house. Perhaps they had been caught at robbery previously. This time, though, they were sure they wouldn't get caught. Standing in a dark street, they were keyed up.

"This is the one," one might have said. "Ain't nobody home. It's pitch black."

"No car in the driveway," said the other.

"They're probably at a New Year's Eve party." They couldn't know that Mama did not drive and therefore did not own a car.

"We gotta be careful," one might have said. "I'll go knock." So the one with the crowbar walked to the front door, gave a sharp knock at the door—five or six sharp raps. He probably jumped over the railing of the porch and slipped around the side of the house.

The noise was loud enough that the next-door neighbors heard something. "We heard a noise," they later told the police, "but it wasn't repeated."

Mama did not answer. She was already asleep. She also had a slight hearing problem. The two youths must have believed the coast to be clear.

The one with the crowbar walked to the back door. His breathing must have come in quick gasps. A quick tap on the glass and a hand snaked through the broken pane. The latch was turned.

He probably stood just inside the door for a minute, straining his ears, listening. He heard the hum of the refrigerator, the tock of the old clock.

He stepped farther in, feeling his way in an unfamiliar kitchen. *Bam.* He stumbled in the dark against the refrigerator, leaving a smudged handprint. He made his way to the front door. He clicked the latch, letting his buddy inside.

Feeling more confident together, they began to ransack the living room and hallway, pulling out drawers and dumping their contents on the floor. Maybe one swore as he scattered objects full of precious memories but worth few dollars.

From behind the one in the hall, a voice must have seemed to jab his adrenal glands. "What are you doing in here?" my mother might have said from the door of her bedroom.

He whirled around. *Oh, no,* he must have thought. *I've been seen.*

This wasn't supposed to happen. This was supposed to be a perfect rob-bery. Where did this old woman come from? This is terrible. She can even recognize me. I'm going to go to jail. This old woman is ruining my life.

He probably glanced down at the crowbar in his hand. Sav-agely he lashed out with the crowbar, slamming my mother across the cheek. She fell backward. He struck again, landing a blow across her shoulders. She tumbled against the wall and landed on her back. He stepped forward and crashed the crowbar into her skull. She lay unconscious, dying on the floor.

He must have experienced extreme anger, guilt, and fear all mixed together. "What have you done?" his partner might have yelled. Perhaps the partner ran out the back door. The first one began to smash objects with the crowbar. He ran to the kitchen and threw objects. "The old woman shouldn't have been here!" he might have yelled. The guilt must have been overwhelming. He couldn't look himself in the face at what he had done. He began to smash every object with a reflecting surface.

"She made me do this." In rage he ran back to my mother's body, holding a wine bottle from the kitchen. He viciously as-saulted her body, thrusting it under her nightgown. She didn't stir. Her breathing was weak. Then, grabbing up a change container, he turned and caught his reflection in the hall mirror. He snatched the crowbar and smashed it. He fled the scene, plans ruined, and overcome with the shame of having murdered.

The house would have been silent except for my mother's weak, irregular breathing. No one could hear her blood draining into the carpet beneath her head and pelvis.

As I traced the likely events of that night in my mind, I felt that I understood better what had happened. The youth who had mur-dered my mom had done a terrible thing—nothing will change that. It was an evil act.

But by recalling the events (as they had been "seen" in my imagination all day), I short-circuited revenge motivations born of rumination and replaced them by empathic recall. It was not an empathy that whitewashed the facts. It was empathy that tried to understand. Through empathizing with what might have been going on in the youth's mind, I understood that he had lashed out in fear, surprise, guilt, and anger. I guessed that he had responded to his own guilt and shame with the destructive anger that he unleashed on the house and my mother's body.

Through empathizing with the youth, I stopped indulging in the desire to kill him or hurt in return, as I had been doing all day. I felt sorry for what he must have experienced and must be experiencing. *He is probably alone,* I thought, *worried about what he's done, sickened by the news reports that Mama died soon after the attack.* I knew that the guilt and shame he had shown in the scene of violence must be a powerful force in his life wherever he was at that moment. I imagined him wrestling with his guilt alone that night, just as I wrestled with my grief. I felt a sense of compassionate understanding for this youth, while still seeing the utter ugliness of what he had done.

As I look back on the experience now and analyze it, I can see that I was experiencing new emotions. Instead of the rage and fear that I experienced before empathizing, I felt compassion. My body was being reprogrammed. The scene, vivid in my mind, was being paired with different events occurring in my body. Different neurochemicals were flooding my brain. I was experiencing different gut feelings. My face softened, my jaw no longer clenched in anger and hatred. Instead of associating the event with a fantasy of revenge, I was associating the event with sadness and compassion for a needy person—a person who needed serious help and who needed to be prevented from hurting others.

At no time in my empathic fantasy did I ever construe his act as being anything but wrong and evil. It was not justifiable. It was not excusable. But after my empathic fantasy, it was more understandable. I thought about what might have been the murderer's experience. I did not merely judge him from outside.

It wasn't easy to force myself to imagine such a traumatic scene. In fact, my mind rebelled against it. I wanted to flee from the thoughts. Yet I knew that I needed to try to understand an act of a desperate human. So I persevered with my imagined scene based on information from police reports. (If I had really thought I was going to be unable to handle this, I would have wanted to dwell on it only with a counselor available.)

> *It wasn't easy to force myself to imagine such a traumatic scene. In fact, my mind rebelled against it. I wanted to flee from the thoughts. Yet I knew that I needed to try to understand an act of a desperate human.*

By forcing myself to imagine this scene and arrive at a compassionate stance, even though the memory was traumatic, the process probably helped speed my forgiveness. Researchers tell us that when people are experiencing a trauma, their memory processes it differently than in nontraumatic conditions. Trauma seems to cause the emotional centers of the brain to become extremely active, and it changes emotional experience strongly. Imagining a traumatic scene and pairing it with the emotion of compassion most likely reprogrammed my emotions of rage and fear more quickly and more powerfully than had I tried to imagine the same scene a week or a month later.

Even though the imagination was difficult, it was, in the long run, good for me. Empathic recall is difficult. It is emotional. Yet empathy helps promote healing.

WHAT YOU SEE IS WHAT YOU GET

Imagine vividly. Empathy is the key step in forgiving. To develop deep empathy, imagine the incident vividly from the point of view of the perpetrator—as I did earlier with my mother's murderer. Picture the scene as clearly as you can. Run a movie through your head. However, instead of seeing the movie from your own point of view, picture it as if you were the person who hurt or offended you. Imagine what you saw (as transgressor). Imagine what you heard, what you smelled, tasted. Make the picture as real as you can. Imagine your thoughts and feelings. What were your motives? Most people do not act from evil motives—although it sometimes seems that way from our point of view. Most people are trying to do what they think is best to meet a perceived need. Later they might look back and see that their decisions were mistaken or self-motivated.

Forgive a difficult person by focusing on symbolic events. When we become unforgiving toward a person, usually it is because we have generalized our opinion from many accumulated hurts. In a good relationship, we are not usually bothered by small or infrequent hurts. But if the number or size of the hurts becomes large enough, we usually jump to conclusions. We move from seeing the relationship as good, the person as trustworthy, and the emotional tone as positive to seeing the relationship as troubled, the person as untrustworthy, and the emotional tone as negative. We whip off the rose-colored glasses and slam the dark glasses in place.

If your relationship with the transgressor has deteriorated to the level of hating the person, you will probably never forgive unless you recall specific events that were hurtful. Recall each event and work through it before going on to the next. Forgiving a *person* requires accumulating forgiveness from several symbolic events.

CHAPTER 3

E: Empathize

We must develop and maintain the capacity to forgive.
He who is devoid of the power to forgive is devoid of the
power to love. There is some good in the worst of us and
some evil in the best of us. When we discover this, we are
less prone to hate our enemies.
— MARTIN LUTHER KING JR.

In Charles Dickens's much-assigned but little-read novel *Great Expectations* lives Miss Havisham. She spent her life in a darkened room, half dressed in her wedding clothes from years before. Her fiancé had sent her a note breaking the engagement as she was preparing to go to the church for their wedding. Time froze for Miss Havisham. From that day forth, she lived in her room with the hands of the clock stopped at precisely the time she received the message. Miss Havisham is a clear picture of unforgiveness. Her growth was stunted by poison from a harm she could not forgive.

Miss Havisham adopted a beautiful young girl named Estelle. Estelle was Miss Havisham's revenge on men. A man had been unjust. Estelle would make men pay. Miss Havisham trained her to lead men on into loving her deeply. At the peak of their love, she struck, casting their love aside. She was a beautiful black widow spider.

Pip, the protagonist of *Great Expectations,* visited Miss Havisham. Miss Havisham began to enjoy Pip's company and like him very much. Of course, Pip fell in love with Estelle, who led Pip on. In front of Miss Havisham, Estelle broke Pip's heart. As Miss Havisham saw his pain, she was moved with empathy. She fell to her knees and asked Pip if he could forgive her for causing him pain. Miss Havisham's empathy was the goal that prodded her to request forgiveness. Her empathy for Pip then helped her to forgive the man who, years before, had rejected her.

LEVELS OF EMPATHY

Empathy can be experienced at three levels[1] (Figure 3.1). At the shallowest level of empathy, you understand the point of view of the other person. At a middle level of empathy, you identify emotionally with the other person, you feel *with* and think *with* the other person. At the deepest level of empathy, you feel compassion as well as emotional identification. This is called compassionate empathy. Each level adds depth to the previous level. If you want to forgive, you must achieve this compassionate empathy.

Recently, I was giving a talk at York University in Toronto. Les Greenberg, a noted researcher of psychotherapy, showed me his lab while I was there. He is interested in *how* people come to forgive people who have deeply wounded them. I saw a videotape of a counseling session with a man who held a deep grudge against both his mother and father. As a ten-year-old boy, he had returned from school to find that his mother had committed suicide. The boy didn't know how to cope all alone. In his ten-year-old mind, his mother had abandoned him. His father, himself overcome

FIGURE 3.1
Three Levels of Empathy

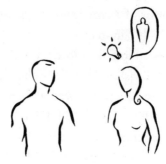

Level 1: Understanding

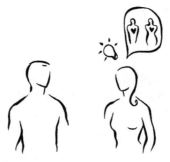

Level 2: Emotional Identification

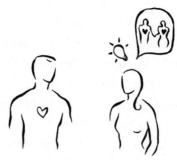

Level 3: Compassionate Empathy

with grief, was depressed, incapacitated, and unable to help. The boy had asked his father, "Don't you love me?" The father's response: "Of course I love you, but you can never love a child like you love a wife."

During the counseling session, I saw the man—now in his thirties—hold his arms wrapped closely around him. "I feel out of touch with the whole human race," he said. "My mother bailed out. My father was never there for me." Within the first fifteen minutes, the man said he was "adrift," "abandoned," and "alone." His most vivid memory was being left "alone in a dark room."

As counseling progressed, he told how his mother abandoned him through her suicide. He'd mentioned this in previous sessions, we learned. Near the end of this session, he suddenly began to talk about his father. His anger toward his father seemed to surprise him. The therapist asked him to pretend to talk to his father. "Imagine your father seated in this empty chair." The therapist pulled a chair directly in front of the man. "What would you like to say to him? Tell him how he abandoned you."

"You were never there for me," he began. "I don't even know if I could talk to you." He looked stonily at the empty chair.

After a silence, the therapist urged, "Give it a try."

"It's not that you weren't there. You weren't there *for me*. You came home at night, but you were always thinking of work. Your body was there, but your mind was not. That's the way you always were. Cold. Detached. I was a nuisance to you. An obligation. I felt like you resented me."

The client poured out his unforgiveness. He was angry, bitter, and full of hate. Then he was fearful of rejection. He whined. Sadness replaced the fear. It finally gave way to a cynical rejection.

One transgression is hard to forgive. How could this man forgive a person who had transgressed many times? How could he forgive a lifetime of drifting alone, out of touch but not out of sight of the person who should have been giving him love and comfort?

"Can you think of one time that stands out?" asked the therapist.

"Playing in the band was my salvation," he said after a moment's thought. "I threw myself into music. I can understand how you never could come to our concerts. Even when I played the solo at the spring concert in my junior year, you didn't come. You said you had a date. You said, 'You understand, don't you?' I said, 'Sure,' but I didn't really. I know it sounds like nothing now, but it was important to me then. It sums up our so-called relationship. You were always somewhere else. I had no mother, and you could never be my father. You were just a biological sperm donor. I never could tell you that. I could never get close enough to tell you."

Anger and hurt competed in the client's face. Hurt seemed to be winning as he gazed in silence at the empty chair.

"What do you think your father's reaction would be?" asked the therapist after the client poured out the litany of his complaints and feelings of abandonment. "Sit in his chair and talk about how he might feel."

The man moved to the father's chair and began to talk for his imagined father. He said, "I'm so sorry, so sorry. I had no idea you were so hurt. So alone. I was hurt by your mother's death and struggled to cope. I simply had nothing left to give to you. I wanted to be a real father to you. I didn't want to add more hurts to you. I knew you were suffering. I just didn't have what it took to give you what you needed. I knew that concert was important to you. There was no excuse for not going. I'm sorry, so sorry."

"What do you want to say to your father now?" asked the therapist.

The client changed chairs. He said, "I'm sorry too. I see now that you did all you could—all you were capable of. I was only ten when Mom died. I didn't understand. You were wrapped up in your own hurt. I condemned you for that. When I was ten, that made sense. Now I'm an adult and I still have not been able to get past my own hurt. I see now that if we are ever going to be back in touch, I need to reach out to you and not wait for you to reach out for me. I'm not ten anymore."

When I saw this case, I was impressed at how much the forgiveness session using two chairs resembled the Pyramid Model to REACH Forgiveness. The client recalled (R) a specific hurt. He literally sat in his father's chair and acted out an empathic (E) response. He had to "be" his father. When he was saying, "I'm sorry, so sorry," he felt sorry. Those feelings were like shovels that turned over the soil, covering some of the acrid, hurtful parts of his own experience. Through empathy, he saw his own shortcomings. As we'll discuss later, he then came to an altruistic (A) forgiveness. He saw how he and his father were alike. That helped him commit (C) to forgive.

For years, using the empty-chair technique, Les Greenberg has been investigating how people resolve unfinished business.[2] The empty-chair technique is a concrete example of empathy in action. When a person sits in the perpetrator's chair, talks like the perpetrator, and explains things from the perpetrator's point of view, then the person must identify with the perpetrator.

To achieve the first level of empathy, the person tries accurately to portray the thoughts and emotions of the perpetrator. To achieve the second, the person literally feels with or thinks with the perpetrator. Whether forgiveness occurs, though, seems to depend quite a lot on whether the person can move to the third level of empathy. Can he or she develop compassion for the one who did the wounding? Can the person care for the wounder? Realize at the gut level that he or she and the transgressor are the same under the skin? If the person cannot feel such compassion, he or she experiences no emotional change and remains glued to unforgiveness. Only after achieving compassion can forgiveness take place.

Greenberg, and now Wanda Malcolm, one of Greenberg's former students, have found that when the person portrays the perpetrator gently and with compassion, the person might soon forgive. But when the person remains hard toward the perpetrator, he or she probably will not forgive—at least not until his or her feelings change. Accusing the perpetrator helps resolve anger by leading to an affirmation of the self and one's rights. But it does not lead to forgiving. Therefore in psychotherapy, empathy has been shown to be a key component in whether people can forgive.

Pay attention to other people's empathy. Empathy can be contagious. Seeing another's empathy can help you heal your own hurts. Richard and Joan married in their forties—both for the first time. Six months later, they were in counseling talking of divorce. Richard was into computer programming. He was logical, hardwired to argue. Joan was into art. She was passionate, feeling slights as though they were deep wounds.

Before one session, Joan had to work late; boss's orders. She phoned me and told me to start the session with Richard. She would join us late.

Richard began to complain that Joan refused to understand him. "No matter how I try to tell her about my needs, she won't listen," he said.

"So you don't feel like she listens to you."

"She doesn't. She is always working her agenda."

"That feels devaluing—like she could care less about you."

"Right. I get angry. We end up yelling."

"So you don't feel that she is really hearing you. You feel she doesn't care. That makes you angry, and you express the anger."

"Both of us do. It's not just me. We yell at each other."

"So something makes her angry?"

"Well, I had been thinking more about me, but now that you mention it . . . yeah, I guess she probably doesn't feel like I understand her either."

"Do you?"

"Yes. At least I think so. Maybe I don't. I don't know. She would probably say I don't understand her."

"Do you think I understand how you feel?"

"Yes," he said.

"Why do you think I understand?"

"Because you listen. You sort of repeat back what I tell you and then expand it."

"So when I repeat back what you tell me, it doesn't leave you puzzled about whether I heard you. I tell you what I heard. Then you feel understood."

"Right."

"If I didn't tell you that I understood by summarizing what you say, would you know that I understand?"

"Maybe. I might be able to read it in your face. I guess it would be harder. I might misread you."

"So let's get back to you and Joan. She doesn't seem to understand you, and you think she might not feel understood. If she felt understood by you, what effect do you think that would have?"

"We probably wouldn't get angry as often. She might even be more willing to listen to me. Maybe."

"So if you want her to listen better to you, what can you do?"

"Maybe it would help to assure her that I understand what she's saying. It might not help at all, but hey, that would be no different from now."

Later that hour, Joan arrived. She was frustrated that her boss had kept her late. She began blowing off steam.

"I didn't need this hassle today," she said. She turned to Richard. "I wanted to talk about whose parents we visit over the holidays. I know we'll argue about it. I hate to start out already mad."

I could almost see Richard thinking about our earlier conversation. He had an I-*want*-to-be-empathic look, but did not seem to know exactly what to say.

"I know you're frustrated," he said. "I don't want to jump in with my two cents on the holidays. I really want to hear what your feelings are."

Joan's mouth literally fell open. Richard's openness was so different from his usual logical, argumentative style that she could hardly take it in. She looked to me. "What did you feed this guy before I got here?"

Richard and Joan said the following talk was the best conversation they had had since they were married. Both felt understood.

Richard saw my empathy for him, and he felt more empathy for Joan. Joan saw Richard's empathy for her, and she returned empathy.

Hold On Just a Minute

I have moved fast. Let me summarize. Forgiving depends on feeling differently about a person who hurts or offends you. If you can light that spark of positive feeling—empathy, compassion, or love—it can blaze into forgiveness. Sometimes, as the positive feelings build, the negative voices whisper again in our ear. If we are to forgive, we need to talk back to those doubts.

Forgiving depends on feeling differently about a person who hurts or offends you. If you can light that spark of positive feeling—empathy, compassion, or love— it can blaze into forgiveness.

I'm the victim here. He [or she] should be empathizing with me. It is hard to get into the mind of one who hurt you. That is especially true if the hurt left lasting damage that you face every day. A man looks in the mirror and sees a body damaged in an accident with a drunk driver. He thinks, *I'm the victim. Why should I try to understand the idiot who maimed me?* Daily his unforgiveness allows the driver to reinjure him. She keeps torturing him with his own hatred. The hatred makes him bitter. Someday it could cause a heart attack. Yes, he is the victim, but by holding on to hatred he allows himself to remain a victim.

I don't want to empathize with him. As flickers of empathy for my mother's killer sparked in my mind, objections tried to pour cold water on them. *If I understand the killer,* I thought, *would I be betraying my mother?* I had to ask myself, "What did my mother teach me? Did she teach me to hate?" If I bent under the weight of pressure to hate, *that* would betray my mother. By doing the hard thing—looking the killer in the face and trying to understand—I was honoring her.

If I empathize, that's the first step down the path to forgetting, and I don't want to forget what they did! My wounded heart wants to remember. The truth is that if I succeed at empathizing, I might forgive. Instead of ruminating, I might come to feel closure. I will *not forget.* I will *remember differently.* Because I forgive, I want to combat crime and murder more, not less. When I felt unforgiveness toward the killer, I wanted to bash him. I wanted to add to society's violence. When I forgave, I wanted to stop the crime, stop the senseless murders.

By empathizing with the killer, we forget the victims. Not true. I empathized with my mother while understanding her killer. Those were not polar opposites. Empathizing with one person does not mean we cannot empathize with two, or three, or one hundred others. In fact, I want to understand and feel compassion for all people.

I can't empathize with that! When we are horrified by an act, our entire being rebels against understanding it. How can I empathize with a man who sexually molests his child? How can I understand a serial killer? How can I feel what a torturer feels? Sometimes my mind will not let me think about such evil crimes. In those times, I try to sympathize. I think, *How horrible it must be to have a conscience so seared by hate that he could molest his child. How terrible to feel compelled to kill person after person until forcibly stopped. How tragic to torture another person.* The fact is, no one can empathize with every horrid human act. When my empathy fails, I fall back on sympathy.

But empathy is hard. Too often I give up easily on doing what is hard. I often don't want to try to empathize. I say "I can't" when I mean "It would make me strain." I say "I can't" when I mean "I don't see how I can empathize." Yet there are some things I can do to help me empathize.

Understanding People—
The First Step of Empathy

Before trying to understand the person who might have hurt you, let's set the backdrop. Here are some things to consider.

SOFT EMOTIONS OFTEN HIDE BEHIND HARD EMOTIONS

Underneath any attack is often a sense of fear, stress, worry, and hurt. Attacks are often attempts to achieve goals. When people fear they cannot reach a valued goal, they get angry. They might use anger to bluff others into meeting their goals. They might use anger to drive others away. They might attack because they do not feel powerful enough to achieve goals without using force or intimidation.

Underneath any attack is often a sense of fear, stress, worry, and hurt.

So when a person attacks me, I usually picture the person not as a powerful, strong intimidator, but rather as a person who is needy, afraid, or weak. Seeing the soft-side underneath the strength helps me to understand that this person might need what I can offer—understanding and perhaps forgiveness.

PEOPLE ARE INFLUENCED BY SITUATIONS

People react strongly to situations. Most people are familiar with Stanley Milgram's classic set of experiments in the late 1960s and early 1970s concerning obedience.[3] Milgram told participants he was studying the effect of punishment on learning, but he was really studying participants' obedience to authority.

A white-coated "experimenter" directed a "teacher" (the true participant) to deliver increasingly strong electric shocks to a "learner" (really a confederate of the experimenter). The "experimenter" could only mildly coax the "teacher" to deliver shocks; he could not force the "teacher" to administer them. He said things like, "The experiment requires you to continue." (Of course, no real shocks were delivered.)

Even when the "teacher" heard the "learner" yell in pain and beg to stop, the "teacher" still knuckled under to the "experimenter's" coaxing. In over half of the cases, the "teacher" shocked the suffering "learner" even when the label beneath the switches read Danger XXX.

Milgram found that regardless of the "teacher's" personality traits, race, intelligence, nationality, profession, religion, or any of a host of other characteristics, people zapped the victim simply because someone told them to. It might sound as if people are naturally cruel. Not so. Milgram concluded not that people are wolves but rather that they are sheep. That is, people aren't evil at heart. They're sensitive to social pressure.

Understanding that people react strongly to situations can help us forgive. We usually think of people who have hurt us as evil people. We see them in black capes, intent on inflicting pain. In most cases, though, people are simply caught up in the situation. They are swept along without being able to resist, as were Milgram's participants.

> *We usually think of people who have hurt us as evil people. We see them in black capes, intent on inflicting pain. In most cases, though, people are simply caught up in the situation.*

PEOPLE ARE HARDWIRED FOR SURVIVAL

People react automatically to some stimuli. For example, a man lounging in a chair on a tropical island might never have seen a tarantula. However, if he notices a quick wiggling and a dark shape on his or her sleeve, he will slap at it. He might dive to the sand, heart pounding. Whether the shape was really a tarantula or a dark leaf does not matter. The automatic reaction is fear. Our brains are hardwired for survival. Fear and anger are natural responses when we feel threatened. It is easier to understand transgressions when I see how people can attack me when they feel I have threatened them—whether I have really done so or not.

PEOPLE ARE CONDITIONED BY PAST EXPERIENCES

Sometimes, people have become conditioned by their past to react in fear and anger. One only has to think of the child whose parent strikes him or her occasionally. If the parent moves his or her arm quickly and the child flinches, we can easily see how the child has been conditioned. The child does not think. The child reacts. People who hurt or offend us often do so because they're conditioned by their past. It's easier to understand attacks when I consider how quickly people can be conditioned.

PEOPLE DON'T THINK THINGS THROUGH WHEN HURT

When I am hurt or offended, I want to lash back. Those feelings can be a cue to think empathically. See the box on page 76 for some suggestions about what you might do. Why might the person have hurt me? Is he or she covering vulnerability, responding to the situation, trying to survive, or reacting to a painful past?

What to Do When You Feel Attacked

- Don't react. Instead of letting your own feelings rule, *think.*
- Question why this might have happened.
  > Could the person's fear, stress, worry, or hurt have provoked the attack?
  > Is the person caught up in the punch and counterpunch of the situation?
  > Is the person feeling that you are somehow threatening his or her survival?
  > Is the person reacting more to his or her own painful past than to you?
- If you have already lashed back, can you do anything to lessen the tension?
  > Can you apologize quickly before things get out of hand?
  > At a minimum, even if you believe the attack was not provoked, can you say, "I am not trying to make you angry. I don't want us to argue"?
  > Before you respond with your own side of the argument, can you listen thoroughly to the person and summarize his or her point of view?

Perhaps the person is reacting. There's no planned hurt, just punch and counterpunch. In the midst of an argument, a friend might say something that deeply hurts or offends. *Give her a break,* I might think. *I act without thinking at times too.*

If the offense seems more deliberate, try to get into the offender's mind. Most people want to get along more than they want to fight with someone else. Therefore, when someone seems to pick a fight or hurt you intentionally, usually it's because he or she feels unable to get along with you. Ask yourself, "Why is he or she acting this way?" That question is the beginning of empathy.

Sometimes we can ask people tactfully what they are experiencing. We might say, "When you yelled at me, I felt like I made you angry. Did I do something that made you angry?" Getting the other person's perspective directly can help you forgive.

How to Empathize

A general understanding of people takes us only to the threshold of empathy. To empathize, we must discern why *this person* has hurt *me* in this way.

WRITE A DESCRIPTIVE LETTER

Write a letter as if you were the person who hurt you. Explain your offender's motives, thoughts, and feelings. Sure, you might be guessing. You can't know exactly why he or she hurt you. Or the person might have revealed only a part of what he or she was experiencing.

> *Write a letter as if you were the person who hurt you. Explain your offender's motives, thoughts, and feelings.*

You know how strong situational pressures can be. (Remember Stanley Milgram's studies.) So pay careful attention to what the person saw or might have seen or heard. What did you do that could have been misperceived?

Remember, write the letter as if you were the transgressor. I got this suggestion from my son, Jonathan, who was giving advice to his sister Becca.

"Why do you think Joanie was gossiping about you?" he asked her.

"I don't know. I can't understand how she could stab a friend in the back."

"Have you tried?"

"No."

"Why don't you pretend to be Joanie and write yourself a letter? Explain yourself as Joanie. Maybe you can figure how to talk to Joanie if you can understand what might have made her gossip."

Becca scribbled out some quick notes. She and Joanie patched up the break. It worked!

Here is another example. Suppose Louise, a coworker, has offended Ralph by criticizing Ralph's work to the boss. Ralph has been struggling all week to forgive Louise. He decides to write a letter as a way to understand Louise. He writes this.

> *Dear Ralph,*
>
> *I wanted to help you understand why I criticized your portfolio to the boss. I hope this helps you eventually forgive me. I know there is no excuse for putting down your work, so I'm not trying to make light of my actions or justify myself. I just want to tell you how I experienced things.*
>
> *The boss came in looking for you on Tuesday. He was holding your portfolio. He seemed excited. "Isn't this great?" he said.*
>
> *"Yes, it is," I said. "Ralph did a good job of collecting all the facts and organizing them."*
>
> *"I'm really glad that somebody around here is on the ball," he said. I suppose I felt criticized when he said that.*

Anyway, a few minutes later, at my earliest opportunity, I mentioned the project I put together last week. He sort of waved his hand like he was brushing away a pest, and said, "Yes, but this job of Ralph's was superb."

I was so put out, I blurted out without thinking, "Well, I don't think he included the Sanchez or Mendel figures."

The boss looked down at the report and flipped through some pages. He turned and went back to his office.

I felt badly about pointing out the omissions. I didn't mean to get you in trouble. I suppose my own ego was hurt, and I was trying to show him how smart I was. I really wasn't aiming to get you in trouble at all. I was horrified when you came and were so angry with me.

I'm really sorry.

—Louise

Remember, Louise didn't really write the letter. In fact, she might actually have had more sinister motives than Ralph gave her credit for. By trying to get into Louise's head, though, Ralph forced himself to see motives other than those he had been thinking about.

WRITE A LETTER OF APOLOGY

In our workshops, we ask people to write an empathic letter from the viewpoint of the offender. Sometimes we get this: "I am so sorry for hurting you. I am such a jerk for calling you names. I am scum. I deserve to be chewing gum stuck to the bottom of your shoe. I want to eat worms and live in a cave as the punishment that I deserve, as dung, for having offended you."

This is an apology, not a letter of empathy. The fantasized, overdramatized apology from the offender is a kind of harmless justice. People who have been hurt fantasize the offender lowering himself or herself. That balances the scales a bit, reducing unforgiveness. It makes forgiving easier. We want people to write only the empathic letter, but when people do write an apology letter, we don't correct them. The letter does help a little.

The fantasized, overdramatized apology from the offender is a kind of harmless justice.

The I-am-scum letter works for another reason. The letter of fantasized apology helps change the mood. It's hard to write the I-am-scum letter without bringing humor to the situation. Recall, forgiveness is replacing the unforgiving emotions with other emotions. Humor works. People lighten up. Forgiveness can begin.

MAKE AN AUDIOTAPE

Some people have a hard time writing letters. We ask those people instead to make an audiotape imagining the motives, thoughts, feelings, and situation of the transgressor. Once they narrate the letter, they play it back. In listening, they feel empathy. Sometimes, even if they cannot feel empathic, they can confront the bitterness and resentment revealed by the audiotape.

EMPATHY FOR TECHIES

People who tell me they cannot write letters often write thirty e-mails a day. I suggest they write an empathic e-mail to themselves as if they were the transgressor. If you're a maestro at the keyboard, sit at your computer and compose. Then delete the e-mail.

FOR THE POETIC

Some people write expressive poems. They can reveal deep feelings in unrhymed verse. Instead of writing about their own feelings, however, they write from the point of view of the transgressor. Is expressive poetry for you? Try it.

TALK TO A FRIEND

If you love to talk, grab a close friend and have a cup of coffee. Explain that you want to understand the person who hurt you. Talk with your friend as if you were the transgressor. You won't have quite as much control as writing a letter, e-mail, or poem or narrating an audiotape. Your friends will probably support you, taking your side against the person who hurt you. Unfortunately, instead of moving you toward forgiveness, talking to a well-meaning friend can sometimes actually move you farther from forgiveness. It can entrench you in blame. Sometimes, though, a friend can be a great sounding board to bounce your reflections off, which can promote empathy.

CREATE YOUR OWN EMPTY-CHAIR THERAPY ROOM

Maybe you want to be your own therapist. Remember Les Greenberg's empty-chair conversation. Set up two chairs in the privacy of your own home. Pretend that one chair is occupied by the person who hurt you. Sit in the other chair. By switching chairs and talking for each person, you might become more understanding, empathic, and ready to forgive.

LISTEN TO THE TRANSGRESSOR'S STORY

Lastly, you can develop empathy for the person who hurt you if you listen, really listen, to the other person's story of hurts. Erwin

Staub has people in Rwanda share their stories of pain and hurt. The embattled Hutus and Tutsis are brought together in a circle. Even years after the massacres, they're not ready even to hear the word *reconcile,* much less *forgive.* But when they're able to listen to each other, they develop a sense of empathy for others. Empathy begins with understanding another person's story. It spreads to two people. Then to the other group. In South Africa, the Truth and Reconciliation Commission used the same principle. Victims of apartheid- or rebellion-inspired violence wanted to tell their stories of victimization. Thousands of tearful stories were told at the human-rights hearings.

Victims also wanted to hear the perpetrators' stories. Many wanted to see perpetrators of violence brought to justice. Many just wanted to hear the words "I'm sorry." As testimonies unfolded from perpetrators, two styles seemed to emerge. Some defiantly confessed their deeds. Like the Nazis long ago during the Nuremberg trials, they denied responsibility. Others confessed and said those healing words, "I'm sorry." When regret was sincere, many victims rushed to forgive.

Forgiving started with hearing one story. It grew to two. Then to more.

Rosalie Gerut is a Jewish adult child of a Holocaust survivor. She grew up in a home full of stress, which came from her parents' having survived the camps in which six million Jews, more than three million Russians, and people from numerous other groups (such as Gypsies, the infirm, and the elderly) were cold-bloodedly slaughtered under the orders of the SS. Rosalie's great insight was to realize how much the families of SS soldiers suffered. She found them riddled with guilt and shame. Children of SS soldiers were horrified at what their fathers had done. Rosalie cofounded an organization named One by One. She brings first-generation survivors of the Holocaust and first-generation family members of Nazis together to hear each other's stories. They empathize one by one.

Meetings are risky for both sides. When people are vulnerable, they can be hurt easily. If they can get past being defensive, if they can listen—really listen—they can feel empathy. One by one, they can begin to consider forgiveness.

> *Meetings are risky for both sides. When people are vulnerable, they can be hurt easily. If they can get past being defensive, if they can listen—really listen—they can feel empathy. One by one, they can begin to consider forgiveness.*

If you listen to the person who hurt you talk about his or her own hurts, you might begin to feel empathy for the person. This, of course, is the most risky of all the attempts to empathize. It assumes that you will not be further victimized, that you can listen without being provoked, and that you can control your urge to strike back or be defensive. Not easy tasks.

THE IMPORTANCE OF EMPATHY

Empathy is important for forgiveness to take place. The movie *Regarding Henry* stars Harrison Ford as a hard-driving, obnoxious, self-interested lawyer. One night when Henry goes to the store, he blunders in on a robbery and is shot in the head. The head trauma doesn't kill Henry, but it changes his personality, making him a less aggressive, gentler person.

Henry tries to adjust to his new life, but he has no memory of his past. Learning to live with his wife again is a challenge. While she remembers the old Henry, he doesn't remember her. His love for her reblooms. Then, he discovers that she had been unfaithful to him before his head injury. Henry is devastated, wounded, betrayed. He is utterly unforgiving toward her.

Then he finds that he himself had an affair. By discovering his own weakness, he finally empathizes with his wife's weakness. Only then does he forgive her for her infidelity. Empathy did not force him to forgive. But it required the humility of knowing he and she were the same under the skin. They could cry the same tears, feel the same regret, mourn as love felt like it was sliding between their fingers. They could work together in an alchemy that produced pure gold of the soul. In Chapter 4, I will discuss the humility needed to move up the Pyramid Model to REACH Forgiveness.

Can You Apply What You Have Learned?

Earlier you selected several transgressions you wanted to try to forgive. Can you apply what you have learned to each of those? Can you write an empathic letter, make a tape, or talk to an empty chair in each transgression? If you can, it will help you really forgive.

You will learn whether you can forgive those hard-to-forgive hurts only if you spend the time empathizing. Whether you empathize right now, in your chair tomorrow before work, or in the morning before little feet begin to scurry around the house is unimportant. That you commit to think, write, and *feel* is crucial.

So if you have the time, turn the book back to the sections on how to empathize. Think of the examples you picked in

Chapter 1 (or peek back at what you wrote). Then commit yourself to empathizing. Think seriously about when you can set aside time to reflect and empathize, and start the process. Then press on to the centerpiece of the Pyramid Model to REACH Forgiveness—how to give that altruistic gift that is for giving.

✳

CHAPTER 4

A: Altruistic Gift of Forgiveness

Of some thoughts one stands perplexed—especially at the sight of men's sin—and wonders whether one should use force or humble love. Always decide to use humble love. If you resolve on that, once and for all, you may subdue the whole world. Loving humility is marvelously strong, the strongest of all things, and there is nothing like it.

—FYODOR DOSTOYEVSKY

Just because I understood the impulses and motives of my mother's murderer did not automatically mean that I would forgive him. I can understand someone perfectly and still think that he or she has committed an unforgivable act. I needed something more to forgive.

What We Found Through Science

In the introduction, I told you about our studies that compared empathy-based forgiveness with self-benefit-based forgiveness.

People in the empathy-based group were able to forgive more deeply and hold on to forgiveness longer than were the people who forgave to benefit themselves, who did better than the people who didn't forgive at all.

Even more interesting, we analyzed individuals within both groups. People who forgave more and whose forgiveness lasted longer were those who felt empathy for the perpetrator, *regardless of which group they were in.* People who did not generate empathy or compassion toward the perpetrator did not forgive, regardless of which group they were in. Even people in the control group forgave if they were able to feel a sense of empathy for the perpetrator. From that study and others, we concluded that if a person did not feel empathy, he or she probably would not be able to forgive.

From that study and others, we concluded that if a person did not feel empathy, he or she probably would not be able to forgive.

Another puzzle arose from our data. Even some people who felt empathy didn't forgive. Empathy is necessary to forgive, but it isn't sufficient. We can understand and empathize with a person who might have robbed us, but we still may harbor a desire for vengeance. Jason found this out in a victim-offender reconciliation program when he met with the man accused of mugging him. The transgressor said, "I'm sorry," but his gaze slid to the side like butter melting on a pan. Jason learned that the man had been raised in a broken home. He had been abused by his stepfather, who would drink heavily and then take out his anger on the man, his younger brother, and his mother. Jason listened to the man's story and halfhearted apology. He felt bad for the man and empathized with him. Yet he wasn't ready to forgive him.

🌿   *Empathy is necessary to forgive, but it isn't suffi-cient.*

Empathy takes us part of the way to forgiveness. What else is needed for forgiveness?

Humility

The answer was brought home dramatically as I recalled that night of forgiveness. I could empathize with my mother's murderer. I could understand how he could feel that his freedom would end because he had been seen. I could even see how a youth who already had an impulse-control problem might strike out with the crowbar without thinking. As I pictured him striking my mom, suddenly my mind flashed back to hours earlier. I had stood with my brother and sister in my brother's back room. I had pointed to the baseball bat and said, "I wish that whoever did this were here. I would beat his brains out."

I had just imagined the scene of gory violence and pain that came from a youth beating my mother with a crowbar. When I remembered how I had wished to do the same thing, even to someone who had done such evil, I knew I had done wrong. True, I hadn't carried out the act like the youth had. But what if the youth had been standing in front of me in my moment of rage? I might have taken the baseball bat and killed him.

The sad truth was the uncovering of blood lust in my heart. I felt that I was no better than the murderer.

In fact, in some ways I felt I was even worse than he. The youth's plans for quick riches had been suddenly interrupted by my mother's appearance. His response was a knee-jerk reaction. On the other hand, I had contemplated my hatred on the seven-

hour trip to Tennessee. All day, as we listened to the detectives unfold the story of the murder, I plotted murder in a vengeful heart.
I thought for a long time about his violence. I could not plead
impulsiveness. Yet I still was willing to do violence to him in retribution for what he had done to my mother.

I felt embarrassed, ashamed, and guilty. That guilt was compounded because I am a Christian. I didn't want to act or even
have motives that dishonored my deep religious convictions. I
could truly sense my kinship with the youth who had done the
terrible crime to my mother. We were blood brothers. I was capable of wanting to murder.

I could be empathic and still judge. When we are wronged, it's
easy to feel morally superior. To forgive, I needed to go beyond
empathy. I did that when I was able to see myself as not so different from the murderer.

It's easier to condemn someone who is totally different from
me than it is to condemn someone who is similar to me. That's
why warring enemies emphasize their differences. That's why we
dehumanize people whom we wish to hurt. We treat them as objects. We think of them as vermin. We want to exact revenge without seeing a bond of similarity. By seeing my own vengeful heart,
I experienced humility. I was able not to feel so superior to the
one who wronged me. I could see, in humility, my kinship to
him.

However, it wouldn't have been helpful simply to stew in my
guilt and self-condemnation. By feeling miserable about my own
imperfections, I would not automatically forgive.

I Needed God's Forgiveness

My guilt immediately triggered the beliefs I had practiced for
years: When we truly feel guilty, rather than condemn ourselves,

we can take our guilt to God, who will forgive. God's love and mercy are the basis of forgiveness. I knew that I could confess my wrongdoing with sincere regret. God was kind and would forgive.

So I prayed to be forgiven of my darkened heart and blood lust toward the youth. I felt God's forgiveness of my hatred and murderous intent. When that happened, a sense of my own receipt of forgiveness flooded me with gratitude.

We Can Recall Others' Forgiveness

For me, my sense of being forgiven was a religious experience. We have found in our research that the same psychological impact occurs when people recall other times when they were forgiven—by humans.

> *For me, my sense of being forgiven was a religious experience. We have found in our research that the same psychological impact occurs when people recall other times when they were forgiven—by humans.*

By now almost two thousand people have gone through our Pyramid Model to REACH Forgiveness. Every one has been able to recall a time when he or she had hurt or offended someone who had forgiven. One group member, Lauren, said, "I rebelled against my parents during high school and college. I told them I was at a friend's house. Instead I shot up on heroin. They trusted me. I told them I was visiting a different church from the one where I grew up. Instead I got high. They trusted me. I told them I was a virgin. I lost it one night at a party when I was drunk. They trusted me. I was living a lie. I hated to be at home because my parents were trusting me.

"In my junior year of college, I told my dad. He was shocked. It was harder to tell my mom because I knew she would judge me. But I couldn't keep living the lies.

"My mom was disappointed. She cried. My dad had been disappointed too, I guess. He seemed to know I didn't need his judgment. He was more accepting of me even though he was hurt.

"For a month, I expected to be disowned. I waited for the angry, judgmental confrontation from my mom. After a month, she drove four hours to my school and was waiting for me on the steps of my apartment when I came back from class. When I saw her sitting there, I almost ran away to hide.

"We went inside. Her first words were 'Honey, I love you so much. You are still my daughter.' We talked for hours.

"I still sometimes get drunk, but at least now I'm not living a lie. My mom and dad both forgave me for lying to them and for disappointing them. The day I knew they forgave me and still loved me was probably the happiest day of my life."

Lauren used the memory of her gratitude at receiving her mother's forgiveness to motivate her to give the gift of forgiveness to the young man who had taken her virginity when she had passed out at a party. That young man needed the forgiveness that only she could give.

So, like Lauren, I felt someone's forgiveness—for me it was God's forgiveness—of my hatred and murderous intent. When that happened, I was flooded with gratitude.

The Gift of Forgiveness

When I had confronted my own dark motives and received the freedom of forgiveness, I came to an inescapable conclusion: If I could be forgiven for wanting to kill someone, couldn't this needy young man also benefit if I forgave him? If I could be forgiven of a heart darker than his, then who was I to withhold my forgiveness from him? I couldn't tell the young man I had forgiven him. However, in my imagination, I could extend a gift to him.

He had damaged my family. He had taken my mother's life. I couldn't undo those losses by hating. He had hurt me by his act. I could do something about that. I knew that this youth *needed* forgiveness. I couldn't withhold what he needed. I forgave. Since then, I have felt peace.

The Surprise of Forgiving

All our positive emotions, such as love, affection, empathy, compassion, pity, and sympathy, are in a tug-of-war with negative emotions such as unforgiveness. When we yield to unforgiveness, it can drag us over the crest of the hill into a free fall of bitterness, resentment, and hatred.

> *When we yield to unforgiveness, it can drag us over the crest of the hill into a free fall of bitterness, resentment, and hatred.*

To win the tug-of-war requires hard emotional work. We cannot see how close we are to the precipice of forgiving. When we step over the edge, though, our momentum pulls the negative emotions into a cool bath of forgiveness. We are surprised by joy. Love is possible again.

> *To win the tug-of-war requires hard emotional work. We cannot see how close we are to the precipice of for-*

giving. When we step over the edge, though, our momentum
pulls the negative emotions into a cool bath of forgiveness.

When we're tortured by unforgiveness and finally are able to grant forgiveness, a transforming surprise occurs. Forgiving is like a flood of light at sunrise. Darkness has covered the sky, but the sun suddenly peeks over the horizon, illuminating giant clouds that stretch high above the horizon. Billowy clouds are lit with orange, red, and purple. The sky is afire with colors. This is the relief of forgiveness after wrestling with unforgiveness.

The Altruistic Gift of Forgiveness

Altruism is unselfish regard for another person. Altruism is giving the other person something simply for his or her own good. We feel good when we act altruistically, but we don't act altruistically to feel good. We act altruistically because it's the right thing to do.

EXAMPLES OF ALTRUISM

O. Henry wrote the brilliant short story "Gift of the Magi." A husband and wife, deeply in love, gave up their most prized possessions to purchase a Christmas gift for each other. The husband sold his treasured watch to purchase beautiful combs for the long, gorgeous hair of his bride. The wife cut off her hair and sold it to purchase a beautiful chain for her husband's watch. Both people gave self-sacrificially and altruistically to bless the other person.

Martin Sheen and Alan Arkin starred in another beautiful story of altruism, *The Fourth Wise Man,* based on Henry van Dyke's novella "The Story of the Other Wise Man." Martin Sheen portrayed a rich physician—one of four magi (wise men)—

who sought to be present at the birth of the Christ child. While he was converting his entire fortune into three precious jewels, the other three wise men set out by camel to follow the star that would eventually lead them to Bethlehem.

Martin Sheen, accompanied by a whiny attendant (Alan Arkin), sold one of three jewels to purchase what he needed to make the journey alone. The fourth wise man happened into Bethlehem as Herod's troops were slaughtering children. The wise man purchased the life of one child with the second of his three jewels.

Sheen and Arkin stumbled into a leper colony. The fourth wise man agreed to stay, using his medical training to help the lepers, "just for one day." One day turned to two, which turned to years. Still, the wise man hoped someday to see Jesus to give him the final jewel.

When the very existence of the colony was threatened, the fourth wise man offered to trade his final jewel for seeds to sustain the colony, but his loving friends refused his sacrifice. However, he used the final jewel to purchase freedom for a friend's daughter who was being taken away into slavery. He had given away the last of his fortune. Thirty or so years from the story's start, the fourth wise man had devoted all of his fortune and even his health to the unselfish service to others.

One day, word arrived: Christ had come to Jerusalem. A blind friend of the wise man had been healed. "Come. Let us go see him," said the friend.

In the most poignant moment of the film, the fourth wise man looked at his destitute surroundings, felt his weak, work-worn heart, and—after having poured out his life for others—said in true humility, "But I have nothing to give him."

Altruism is other-oriented love. Often, altruism is thought to be tainted if it isn't self-sacrificial, or if the giver derives some benefit from an act. But benefits that flow from loving acts are inevitable. Love given is love returned. Altruism isn't giving without getting anything in return. It is simply giving for the benefit of the other person.

Altruism isn't giving without getting anything in return. It is simply giving for the benefit of the other person.

Three Parts to the Altruistic Gift of Forgiveness

Helping people give an altruistic gift of forgiveness to one who has harmed them consists of three distinct acts: guilt, gratitude, and gift.

GUILT

In our research, we ask people to recall an incident in which they did something that was wrong even though they knew it was wrong, yet the person whom they offended or hurt granted them forgiveness. At first, people may recall trivial times when they were forgiven. When I began to think of times in my past that I had offended or hurt someone and had been forgiven, I first recalled a night my brother and I were doing the dinner dishes. Mike was washing. I was drying. As we often did when young, we were teasing each other. As I would walk over to pick up the dishes, Mike would flick soapy water on my face. I would snap him with the dish towel. We continued this bantering, but I tired of it before

Mike did. I warned him. When he flicked water one time too many, something snapped (not my towel). I had been sipping Coke from a bottle. (Those were the days—five cents deposit per bottle.) I simply turned the Coke bottle upside down in his pocket. As the Coke ran down his leg, the shocked look on his face was extremely gratifying (for me).

But I had acted out of proportion to the transgression. I felt guilty. Also concerned. Mike could have held a grudge. He could have poured Coke on me after I went to sleep that night. He did neither. He forgave me, and the War of the Coke Bottles was terminated quickly. I was grateful for his forgiveness.

As we reflect back on our years growing up, numerous examples of receiving forgiveness come to mind. In fact, we have never had a person who could not eventually come up with several examples of times when they wronged someone and were forgiven. Even recalling a trivial example like the War of the Coke Bottles can trigger memories of dozens of such incidents.

More serious than the War of the Coke Bottles, I hurt and worried my father by my behavior on a summer job. After my sophomore year in college, I got a job driving a truck. I drove all night, delivering newspaper bundles to carriers throughout east Tennessee. Honestly, I was a terrible driver. I promised my father that I would drive carefully. (I would have told him I would fly if it convinced him to let me take the job.) As soon as I was behind the wheel, predictably, I put the pedal to the metal.

I was late getting home one morning. I was just outside of Athens, Tennessee, about sixty miles away from Knoxville. I was standing on the accelerator. I was probably making about eighty miles per hour when I entered a curve. I could barely hold the truck on the road. Tires were squealing. I was fighting with the steering wheel when I glanced out the window at an oncoming car. It was a black 1959 Ford—the very kind that my father drove. I muscled my way out of the other car's lane, and I looked down at the other car as it went past. My worst fears were realized when I saw the upturned face of my father looking at me. Dread overcame me. I immediately slowed to fifty-five miles per hour. All the way home, I anticipated a stern lecture when he next saw me. My best hope was that he wouldn't force me to quit the job. I expected to be grounded until I received my first Social Security check.

That night, sitting at the table, he spoke as I poured myself a soda. "That looked a lot like you in that delivery truck early this morning."

"Yes, I was finished with work and heading home," I said.

"You seemed to be struggling to hold the truck on the road."

"I guess I was going a little too fast."

"Your mom and I would both be very sad if you were killed in an accident."

"It wouldn't exactly make my day either," I said.

"I won't say anything to your mom. It might worry her. But be careful, will you?"

"I will."

I turned away absolutely surprised. He hadn't even been critical. My relief was almost a physical release. I had known I was in trouble. Suddenly, I was free.

Cokes in the pocket are mild offenses. Reckless driving is more serious. My blood lust to kill the youth who murdered my mother was dead serious. To forgive the last, I had to remember how often my own guilt had been forgiven.

GRATITUDE

Simply recalling events in which we were forgiven, though, isn't enough to make us yearn to grant the gift of forgiveness to one who offended us. In our groups, we ask people to describe their feelings after they knew they had been forgiven. People's responses are remarkably similar. "When I knew I had been forgiven, I felt as if a giant weight had been taken off my shoulders." "I felt free." "I felt that the chains that had imprisoned me in hatred were cut." These are the feelings of gratitude. Gratitude lifts us.

> *"When I knew I had been forgiven, I felt as if a giant weight had been taken off my shoulders." "I felt free." "I felt that the chains that had imprisoned me in hatred were cut." These are the feelings of gratitude. Gratitude lifts us.*

Gratitude or thanksgiving can be simple or complex. Simple gratitude is that feeling of freedom from having received a no-strings-attached gift. If you want to forgive, try to recall a time when you were forgiven as a gift—no strings attached.

Sometimes gratitude is more complicated. If you feel that a gift is given grudgingly, it doesn't set you free. It binds. If you feel that a gift is given insincerely or in an attempt to manipulate you, it doesn't set you free. It ties you up in knots of anger.

Try to remember when you received forgiveness as a simple gift. And when you grant forgiveness, treat it as giving a gift from your heart.

GIFT

In our groups, we then invite forgiveness. "You can empathize with the one who hurt you. You have hurt others and have received a gift of forgiveness. You have benefited by forgiveness. Would you like to give such a gift of forgiveness to the one who hurt you?"

Amy was unhappy with her boss. He had been assigned to

write a technical report on the feasibility of a new product line, but because he was busy, he threw her the project. "He pestered me daily to get the report done," Amy said, "but he never lifted a finger to help." When the report was finished, he submitted it to the vice presidents, and not only did they like the analysis, they promoted him to head the production team for the new product.

"All he did was complain about the things he didn't like with the report. Now no one knows that I did the report, and he's off at the new location. I got no credit, only grief. And no one will ever know, because he's gone."

The turning point in Amy's forgiveness came about when the president of her community recreation association thanked her for a report she had submitted on repaving the parking lot. She realized that she had received the accolades for the report, yet she had worked closely with her best friend to compile the report. And Amy had not acknowledged her friend's help. Oops.

Immediately, she phoned her friend and apologized. "No problem," her friend assured her. Then Amy phoned the president of the recreation association to give credit where credit was due. Surprisingly to her, that event helped her to see her former boss as less manipulative and self-serving. She began to forgive him for not giving her credit for the report into which she had poured so much labor.

What If You Don't Want to (or Can't) Give the Gift?

People don't always wish to give a gift of forgiveness to the one who harmed them. Certainly I would never want to coerce or manipulate anyone into forgiving. Only if you give forgiveness freely will it have its best effect on you and on the one you forgive.

Only if you give forgiveness freely will it have its best effect on you and on the one you forgive.

Most people who use the Pyramid Model to REACH Forgiveness, though, are people who want to forgive but cannot. We typically invite the person, if he or she isn't ready to forgive, to retrace the steps of empathy, his or her own guilt over a transgression, and the gratitude that was felt when he or she received forgiveness from someone else. If it is too difficult to reach forgiveness with a particular unforgiven hurt, try it with an easier one. Put the hard one aside until later. Try again tomorrow.

When we try any new skill, it feels awkward. When I began to play competitive volleyball, I felt like a klutz—for a year. Let's face it: I *was* a klutz. But I kept showing up to practice and to games. (Perhaps I'm a slow learner.) One day I hit an actual spike. Once I hit my first spike, the second was easier. The tenth was easy. The key was to ignore my feelings of incompetence and keep practicing. If you want to forgive but cannot, you must keep practicing until forgiving happens.

Humility and Gratitude

Humility and gratitude are at the center of the A step (altruistic gift of forgiveness) in the Pyramid Model to REACH Forgiveness. "Humility is," as theologian Andrew Murray once said, "not thinking less of oneself than one ought. It is not thinking of oneself at all."[1] Humility is an other-oriented emotion. Humility arises from and reinforces a person's sense of empathy. Empathy is also important to feeling gratitude. Gratitude is a feeling of thanksgiving at having received a gift perceived to be altruistic. Gratitude is an extremely complex emotion because it demands sensitivity and empathy from both the gift giver and the gift receiver.

For a gift receiver to feel gratitude, the receiver must perceive the gift as being given altruistically. That requires empathy. The receiver must place himself or herself in the shoes of the gift giver and conclude that the gift giver is unselfishly giving the gift. The complications to feeling grateful that I mentioned earlier are all due to perceiving ulterior motives.

On the other hand, the gift giver must be empathic too. He or she must understand the needs of the receiver if he or she is to avoid offending the receiver by offering an unwanted gift.

Therefore, the transaction of giving and receiving gifts resembles a mating dance of porcupines. The two try to get close enough to have contact, yet possibilities of prickles pop up at every twist and turn.

Humility and gratitude are intimately joined. A humble person is aware of his or her gifts and talents and accepts them. Yet the humble person doesn't believe that those gifts and talents make him or her a better person than others. In fact, the truly humble person rarely compares himself or herself to others. Humility is other-oriented, not self-oriented. Being oriented toward others, a humble person is grateful for what others have done. He or she is grateful to God, to parents, to mentors, to friends. He or she is grateful for the many people who have forgiven him or her. That gratitude is a steam engine that powers a drive to reach out in altruistic love to forgive someone.

Father Elias Chacour sat beside me at a dinner one night. He is one of the most humble people I have ever met. As president of a university, he still finds the time to be a parish priest. Father Chacour is a Palestinian Christian. As a member of two minorities in Israel, he has ample grounds for feeling victimized. Instead he strives to promote reconciliation because he believes that that is the right thing to do. He has turned his beliefs into action to bring people together. To promote practical reconciliation, he founded a university in Palestine with students and faculty who are Christian, Jewish, and Muslim.

When an Israeli terrorist opened fire on Muslims prostrated in worship, spilling the blood of many innocent people, Father Chacour wrote a letter of protest to the Israeli government. Soon afterward, a Palestinian terrorist strapped a bomb to his back and set it off in a marketplace, killing or wounding more than eighty people—mostly Israeli Jews. Father Chacour wrote another letter of protest to the Israeli government. His fair-mindedness is commendable.

His students were not satisfied with his response. He described the incident in a talk at the State of the World Forum in New York in 2000. "My students came to me," he said. " 'Have you become an American?' they accused me. 'When Americans are upset, they write a letter to their congressman. They think they have solved the problem. That is not enough,' my students said.

"My students wanted to show the love that expressed itself in action. I asked, 'What should we do?'

" 'We want to give our blood to help the injured Jews,' said the mostly Palestinian students.

"So I phoned the Israeli government with my request, and they sent fifteen nurses. I was afraid that only fifteen or twenty students would show up, embarrassing the school. I need not have worried. For six solid hours, fifteen nurses pumped the blood of Christian, Muslim, and Jewish students and faculty. Palestinians gave their blood for the Jews.

"We became blood brothers," said Father Chacour, who had written a book about his experiences.[2] "We were not born Jew, Christian, or Muslim," he said. "We were born *babies*."

When we understand—as Father Chacour simply but eloquently said—that we are born babies, that we all bleed blood, and that we experience the same pains and joys, then we have the basis of the empathy and humility we need to forgive.

People are precious. They are precious not because they are dressed like we are or have the same color of skin as we do. They are precious because they are people of potential. Because I am a Christian, I believe that the value of humans derives from being born in the image of God (as do the other two major religions that sprang from Abraham, Judaism and Islam).

Stephen Huang, speaking on behalf of Cheng Yen, founder of the Buddhist Compassion Relief Tzu-Chi Foundation in Taiwan, agrees that people are valuable. "If I had a new thousand-dollar bill, would you want it?" he asked. "What if I wadded it up? What if I threw it on the floor? What if I stepped on it and scuffed dirt from my feet on it? Would you still want it?"

Everyone at his talk still wanted the thousand dollars. "Just because the bill gets dirty and stains any hand it contacts does not affect its inherent value," he said. "People are valuable. They need and deserve our compassionate love."

Religion can divide, but it seems that on this point, many agree—as do many who embrace no religion. Our empathy, humility, and gratitude somehow ennoble us. In so doing, they inspire us to step beyond our own self-interest and give altruistic gifts of love to those in need.

Our empathy, humility, and gratitude somehow ennoble us. In so doing, they inspire us to step beyond our own self-interest and give altruistic gifts of love to those in need.

Giving those altruistic gifts elevates the giver as well as the receiver. Even more surprising, those gifts elevate those who observe.

Marty Seligman, a psychologist of great vision who has served as president of the American Psychological Association, described a course he taught at the University of Pennsylvania. It was on positive psychology. He assigned students to do two tasks—do something fun and do something nice for others.

"One woman was driving her friends home one snowy night," said Seligman. "She said, 'I saw an old woman whose car was stuck in the snow. She was trying to shovel it free. Down the road, one of my friends asked to be let out. I thought he knew a shorter way home. I watched in the rearview mirror as he walked back. When he picked up the shovel, I began to cry.' The woman went on to say," said Seligman, " 'When I had fun, I felt good for a while, but just seeing him help the old woman has made me feel *proud to be a person* all week.' "

There is an ancient Chinese saying:

> *If you want to be happy . . .*
> *for an hour, take a nap*
> *for a day, go fishing*
> *for a month, get married*
> *for a year, get an inheritance*
> *for a lifetime, help someone.*

Forgiving is an altruistic gift you can give to someone who *needs* forgiveness. You don't even need to tell the person you have forgiven. Just change your actions to reflect the altruistic gift you have bestowed.

Applying the Altruistic Gift of Forgiving

If you've been applying what you've read to several of your own relationships that might require forgiveness, you should now pause and remember. Identify at least three incidents where you have been forgiven. Write about each incident.

Think about how you felt when you knew you had done wrong. Remember the guilt, embarrassment, and perhaps shame you felt. Recall how concerned you were over the consequences. Remember how you might have tried to justify your acts even though you knew deep down that you had done wrong. Write about what happened.

Then recall your feelings and thoughts when you were granted forgiveness. Write them down.

What if the person you hurt made you feel guilty? What if you felt manipulated? Do you want to make the person who hurt you feel guilty or manipulated? How could you avoid making him or her feel bad? Try to come up with at least three incidents in your life where you received forgiveness and list those.

Putting It All Together

Now you're armed with three incidents where you could be grateful for having been forgiven. Return to the several incidents where you were hurt and want to forgive. Pick one. Think it through again. Recall the hurt. Don't see yourself as a victim. Don't see yourself as the Avenger.

Now empathize with the person who hurt you. Get inside his

or her head and feel what he or she might have felt. Sense your common humanity with the person.

Then recall a time when you were forgiven. Tell yourself that you can rise above hurt and revenge. You can give a gift of forgiveness to the person who hurt you. Would you like to do that?

CHAPTER 5

C: Commit Publicly
to Forgive

*I am ashamed that my tongue cannot live up to my
heart.*

—AUGUSTINE

Have you ever struggled to forgive someone and finally
emerged from your struggles believing that you had granted
forgiveness only to doubt that forgiveness later? For most people,
such self-doubts about the reality of forgiveness are common.

I was no different from most people. The night I had forgiven
the murderer was an emotional transformation in me. I pro-
foundly *knew* that I had forgiven.

Sometimes, though, I would flash back to the imagined scenes
of violence that I couldn't seem to shake. *Maybe I didn't fully forgive him,* I would think. I could feel the pain during those times.
The loss of my mother was a sense of darkness and emptiness. Did
that mean my forgiveness was bogus? Was it merely self-deception?

Doubts would steal in like an intruder seeking to rob me of
my peace. Growing weary of self-doubt, I decided to combat

those doubts by using some of the methods we had developed in our workshops.

WHEN DO WE DOUBT OUR FORGIVENESS?

When are the times that we are most likely to doubt that we have really forgiven the one who has harmed us? To defeat the enemy, doubt, I had to understand what led to doubt.

Let's assume you've struggled to forgive an acquaintance, Bob, who betrayed a trust. You might not have seen Bob for years. Finally, you believe you've forgiven him.

First, you might doubt your forgiveness if you see Bob again. Seeing him reminds you of the hurt. Memories are linked to the emotions of fear and anger, which are stored in your brain and body. This is especially true if you don't see Bob very often, or if you come upon him unexpectedly without having had the chance to prepare yourself.

Second, you might doubt your forgiveness if you're hurt similarly by someone else. If someone else—let's call her Natalie—betrays your trust in the same way that Bob did, then you might think, *That's the same way that Bob hurt me,* and the new hurt by Natalie triggers a reexperiencing of the old hurt by Bob. Because you feel the hurt from Bob again, you might think that you haven't fully forgiven Bob.

Third, you might doubt your forgiveness if you're under high stress. When you are stressed, old hurts often resurface. You might spontaneously remember how Bob hurt you, because the stress creates emotions in your body that arouse memories and feelings of previous hurts.

Fourth, you might doubt your forgiveness if you were hurt by the same person again. For example, even if you had forgiven Bob for a past betrayal of trust, if Bob insults you tomorrow, you would probably remember how Bob betrayed your trust previously.

LET'S BE GOOD SCOUTS

Life is full of unexpected meetings. No matter how hard we might try to avoid a person, we bump into her, hear her name, see her friend who reminds us of her.

Life is full of rejections. If I flash back to a painful memory every time someone rejects or disappoints me, I might as well not go to work, not marry, and not have children. Life is full of reminders of past hurts.

Life is full of stress. For most of us, life is filled to overflowing with stress. E-mails, Express Mail, faxes, and phone calls demand attention *now*. Change is everywhere, clamoring for attention. Jobs, bosses, friends, and even leisure pull at us from all directions. If stress can trigger the memory of old wounds, I had better learn to deal with the memory, because stress is a given.

Life is full of other encounters with people who have wounded us. In fact, once I'm wounded, the wound can feel like a chewed place inside my cheek. Every time I move my mouth, it brings me back into contact with the teeth that bit me.

The point is, I will surely recall the wounding—many times. If I cannot avoid recalling the wounding, at least I can adopt the Boy Scout motto: Be prepared.

DON'T JUST TREASURE FORGIVENESS IN YOUR HEART

Assume you have moved through the first three steps to the Pyramid Model to REACH Forgiveness. You R, recalled the hurt. You E, empathized with the person who hurt you. You gave an A, altruistic gift of forgiveness. When you forgave, you forgave from the heart. You knew you forgave, but you didn't make a public statement of the forgiveness. Doubts will happen. Did you *really* forgive?

Had I Forgiven My Father?

My father had a drinking problem. He grew up in a coal-mining town in the east Tennessee mountains. He was the son of a railroad man who was killed when my dad was less than three years old. Dad's mother was blind, with three children growing up during the Depression.

Times were tough. My dad was tough. Life encouraged him to be hard and cynical, and he cooperated. He fought. He drank. He also cussed. He kept a lot of his background from us children while we were young.

When I entered junior high, Dad began to drink a lot. (I hope it wasn't my entry into adolescence that provoked the drinking.) With drinking came its brothers—swearing, anger, and simple mean-spirited hurtfulness directed at us children or Mom.

When Dad wasn't drinking, he was kind. But the moments of kindness got rarer as I got older.

I was fortunate. I could escape into extracurricular activities, tournament tennis, working math problems shut away in our cold back room, or running around town with my friends. My brother (four years younger) and sister (nine years younger) were not as mobile as I. They received the lion's share of the fallout from Dad's drinking. While I accumulated many of my own wounds from Dad beginning in my junior high years and lasting until I moved out after college, it was the wounds to my brother, sister, and mother that led to the core of my unforgiveness toward Dad.

I began to do focused research on forgiveness in 1990, which was the year Dad died of cancer. As he saw the approach of his death, he mellowed. Seeing him deal with the ravages of advancing cancer helped me feel more tender toward him.

I was able to think back through the years, recall some of my biggest hurts, and eventually forgive him. I do not believe I fully forgave him until the year after he had died. I heard the bitterness in my voice when I recalled my dad or talked about his death. That pushed me toward serious forgiveness. I worked hard to forgive and finally felt the ocean breeze of forgiveness freshen my bitterness.

I felt free of the venom that had soured me for years. I hoped to remain free.

But too many things reminded me of my dad. If I had a conflict at work, scenes of conflict with my dad would intrude into memory. If one of my children disappointed me, I would remember a similar time when my dad had scolded me.

I had forgiven him, hadn't I?

Hardwired to Remember

Yes, I had fought through to hard-won forgiveness. When I was reminded of past hurts, I no longer felt the resentment, bitterness, hostility, hatred, or anger that I used to feel. I did recall specific events and remember the pain of the hurt. But hurt is not unforgiveness.

Remember in Chapter 1, I defined unforgiveness as the delayed emotions that arise out of vengeful rumination. I was careful to point out that forgiveness does not replace hurtful memories. It replaces the negative emotions attached to the memories.

We are literally hardwired to remember serious hurts or offenses. The first time we touch a stove as a child, it burns us. We are never tempted to rest our hand on a red-hot stove again. The memory of pain is burned into our brain.

> *We are literally hardwired to remember serious hurts or offenses.*

The same thing happens when people hurt or offend us. The hurt is burned into our brains. It becomes part of our wiring. The sight of the person's face, the sound of his or her voice, the acts of harm, the angry and fearful emotions of our immediate reactions, and the experience of the consequences are permanently recorded. It isn't really like storing a program in a computer; it's more like changing the circuitry of the computer. The biochemistry of our brain literally changes. Neurotransmitters, the chemicals that are released into the space between one neuron and the next to create pathways for memories, are coded to be released when we are reminded of a hurtful event. Electrical and chemical signals in our brain run a familiar route. They move through the emotional centers of our brain, not merely through the cortex. In fact, sometimes we *only* have a feeling of pain and cannot remember why. At other times, we have a memory complete with attached emotions.

When we forgive, we cannot stop the memories of the hurt with its attached immediate emotions. We should not want to stop them. They keep us from recklessly trusting where trust might not be deserved. Forgiveness has replaced the second set of emotions that formed due to our rumination. We are freed to experience empathy, love, sympathy, and compassion instead of being bound to hatred and bitterness.

I summarize this in Figure 5.1. A reminder event triggers the hardwired Transgression Loop. Before we forgave, we would have been caught in an Unforgiveness Loop. After emotional re-

FIGURE 5.1
Hurt Does Not Equal Forgiveness

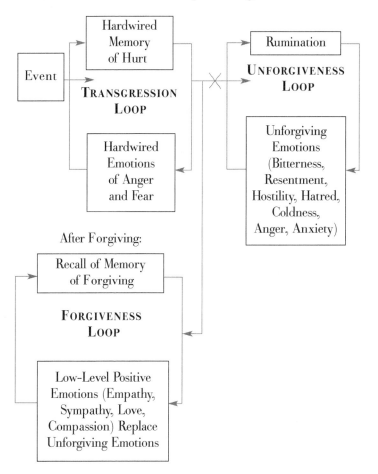

placement of the unforgiving emotions, we can move to a For-giveness Loop.

Now I can remember my father's cruel acts. I can even feel the anger and fear again. But if I don't indulge the Unforgiveness Loop, I can hold on to the forgiveness I worked to experience.

It Is Easier to Doubt When Forgiveness Is Just in My Heart

Forgiveness is an emotional replacement. If I confine my emotions to private feelings, that forgiveness will be fragile. If I wall hard-won forgiveness inside my heart by confining it to a private experience, then doubts can creep in at any moment. But if I do, say, or see something outside of my inner experience to indicate that I have forgiven, it adds other bodily experiences that announce to my brain that I have forgiven. My words and actions become a public record that I have forgiven. It becomes harder to doubt that my forgiveness was real.

> *Forgiveness is an emotional replacement. If I confine my emotions to private feelings, that forgiveness will be fragile.*

To make forgiveness permanent, I want to involve as much of my body and my environment in forgiving as possible. I can do this in four ways. I can be my own behavior therapist, symbolize my forgiveness, write about forgiveness, and tell someone about forgiveness.

Be Your Own Behavior Therapist

DECONDITION YOURSELF

I had forgiven my dad for many of his offenses, but I kept replaying the unforgiveness tape. It was like the I Love You computer virus that fouled computers worldwide in the winter of 2000. Annoying messages replicated out of control. Similarly, my recollections of hurt were intrusive. I needed to do something. I decided to decondition myself.

I sat in my chair and looked at my father's picture. I thought about forgiving rather than condemning him. I repeated this several times daily for a week. Call it boredom or call it deconditioning—whatever happened, I became desensitized to Dad's image. Through sheer repetition, those images lost their sting.

> *I sat in my chair and looked at my father's picture. I thought about forgiving rather than condemning him. I repeated this several times daily for a week. Call it boredom or call it deconditioning—whatever happened, I became desensitized to Dad's image.*

DISCIPLINE YOURSELF NOT TO CRITICIZE

I thought critically of my dad less often after I had deconditioned myself. When I started talking about the past, though, old habits kicked in. I would quickly fall into negative talk, whether to my wife or within my head in that nattering that sometimes passes for thinking. To change, I consciously ordered myself not to criticize. As soon as I would mention my dad, I would try to think, *Don't find fault.*

Old habits, such as speaking critically of Dad, which I had indulged within my family of origin and my marriage, died kicking and screaming in my head. Sometimes I would actually put my hand over my mouth as a reminder not to criticize. Within a year, those habits of a critical tongue were broken. You can stop these thoughts too. If you catch yourself ruminating, tell yourself,

"Let it go," "Don't find fault," "Stop the blame," and change the mental subject. Ask your partner or friend to help you stop those thoughts.

Describe the Positive

There was a lot of good in my father. He (and Mom) raised three responsible and moral children. He must have been doing some things right. I set a goal to replace criticism with thoughts and words of praise.

Even though Dad came from harsh circumstances, he was always responsible. Unable to afford to go to college, he worked long hours as a railroad brakeman and later as a freight conductor. He worked hard on a correspondence degree in accounting, even though he never worked as an accountant. He showed self-discipline in pursuing a degree.

Dad was kind to small children. The neighbors' children loved him. I could see that he gave me, Mike, and Kathy a loving foundation, and he passed along an excitement for learning and an ethic of hard work.

When I decided to rid myself of criticism, I wrote a list of Dad's strengths—much longer than the one above. Then I intentionally practiced thinking of the positive. I knew, of course, that Dad had weaknesses as well as strengths. I had rehearsed the weaknesses for forty-five years. I figured that if I lived to be ninety, I need not be concerned that I had painted too unrealistically positive a picture. Besides, memories of hurts were still triggered at times.

You can create your own list: a concrete reminder to focus on the positive.

Symbolize Your Forgiveness

Washing Our Hands of Judgment

Even before you decide to forgive, you might want to stop judging the other person. Here is an exercise we use in our workshops to symbolize that decision. We have people write a brief summary of the transgression on their palm. They then go to the sink and wash their hands repeatedly until every trace of ink has been washed away. (Hint: Use regular ink, not permanent marker.)

Rock and Roll

Psychologist Rick Marks developed an exercise to help promote public forgiveness based on the biblical story in which town elders caught a woman in adultery.[1] They were about to stone her (the usual punishment for adultery then). Jesus challenged them by writing in the dust and then saying, "Let the one who has not sinned cast the first stone" (John 8:7).

Marks engraved a smooth rock with the words "First Stone." He invites people to respond to those who have hurt them by physically laying down the First Stone. Try this yourself. Go outside and get a large rock. Pick one of the hurts that you identified at the end of Chapter 1. As you think about that hurt, hold the rock in your outstretched hand. Now, while holding it out, think about the weight of your desire for revenge. Feel the stress and pain that holding on to that rock of unforgiveness causes you. When the weight of the desire for revenge becomes so great that you don't want to hold it any longer, you can let the rock fall from your hand as a symbol of your forgiveness. Either let the rock clunk to the floor or deliberately set it down. Feel the relief in your body. That is like the relief of forgiving.

BURNING TO FORGIVE

In our groups, we also invite participants to symbolize their forgiveness in a way that dramatically illustrates forgiveness. They write a brief description of the transgression. Then they burn it and scatter the ashes.

CROSS OUT UNFORGIVENESS

For Christians, the cross is a powerful symbol of forgiveness. I have groups that are composed exclusively of Christians write a brief narrative of the transgression. In prayer they leave it at the foot of a cross.

PATH TO FORGIVENESS

In Judaism, people are admonished to forgive if an offender returns to the path of God. The concept of return, or teshuvah (i.e., repentance), by the offending person frees a victim to forgive. Sometimes, though, the offender's return to the path of God triggers in the victim guilt over feeling unforgiveness rather than freedom to forgive. When this happens, a Jew who wishes to forgive but can't do so can find a path in the woods. He or she can stand on the path while recalling the hurt, but as he or she feels unforgiveness build, he or she can edge off the path.

Standing in the grass, looking down the path that represents the path to God, the victim can walk mentally up the Pyramid to REACH Forgiveness. When he or she feels forgiving, he or she can step back on the path and declare that forgiveness to God.

Use a Cityscape to Remind Yourself of Your Forgiveness

In Islam, one of the ninety-nine qualities of Allah is forgiving. Mohammed, in founding Islam, was ousted from Mecca. When he returned in power to the city of Mecca after eight years of fighting, he practiced forgiveness of his enemies rather than retribution toward them. As a Muslim enters a city and views the skyline, he or she can recall Mohammed's forgiveness in Mecca and use that memory to solidify his or her own forgiveness.

Write Your Forgiveness

Certificate of Forgiveness

When people in our groups forgive, they create a certificate stating the day and time. Sometimes they decorate it. We encourage them to post it on a bulletin board. If the transgression is more sensitive, they can post it inside a drawer.

Below is an example of a Certificate of Forgiveness. Later, if you doubt whether you've forgiven, you can pull out the certificate and look at it and assure yourself that you did.

Write a Letter

Write a letter to the offender. Express your forgiveness of the transgression. Of course, you might not want to send the letter, especially if the person doesn't realize that he or she has done anything to hurt or offend you. Receiving a letter out of the blue forgiving one for having offended a friend is not likely to enhance the relationship.

> ## Certificate of Forgiveness
>
> On March 16, 2002, I decided to forgive my ex-husband, Bill, for the years of neglect and the ugly arguments he provoked as we were headed toward divorce.
>
> I acknowledge that I behaved poorly toward him as well. I hope that someday I might be able to talk with him calmly, express my regret for my part, and ask his forgiveness.
>
> For now, though, I hereby declare that I forgive Bill, and I lay down the weight of my unforgiveness forever, to the best of my ability.
>
> _____
> JEAN HRUSKA

Under conditions of confidentiality, you can read the letter aloud to a friend or valued person in your life. As you read, you hear your own voice proclaiming your forgiveness.

If you have reconciled and have already talked thoroughly with a friend about the forgiveness, you might actually send the letter. But we'll talk more of reconciliation in the second part of the book.

WRITE IN YOUR JOURNAL

If you keep a private journal, write an entry describing your forgiveness. Expressing yourself in a journal can help you deal with difficult events. It can also make you healthier, as research by James Pennebaker has shown.[2] Pennebaker asks people to journal daily for several weeks. They are to express their emotions—

positive or negative. Even though people pour their hearts out on paper instead of to personal friends, the benefits of writing from the heart are great. People heal faster and get ill less often.

WRITE A POEM OR SONG

If you are creative, write a poem about your experience of forgiveness. Perhaps you play an instrument. Put your thoughts and feelings to music.

Tell Someone About Forgiveness

TELL YOURSELF

Say aloud that you have forgiven the person for a particular offense. Just hearing yourself say the words adds another pathway for forgiveness in your brain and body.

TELL A TRUSTED FRIEND

Talk about having forgiven the person who hurt you with a trusted friend or family member. Resolve to maintain that forgiveness. Talking about your forgiveness with a loved one or partner can not only solidify your resolve to hold on to that forgiveness, but also reassure you that you have forgiven.

The night that I forgave my mother's killer was extremely emotional. My experiences were very private. I was sad over the loss. I was traumatized by the violence. But I felt free of unforgiveness. The pain of the loss was too great to talk about forgiveness during the first week after her death. A week later, when the funeral service had taken place, my mother's body buried, and affairs of the estate put into motion, I returned to Richmond. After arriving home, I began to talk about the murder with my wife,

Kirby. I trusted her to understand my struggle with forgiveness and to appreciate that I could grant forgiveness to that youth. I knew that she would understand that I felt I could honor my mother's life more by forgiving, as Mom had taught me, than by holding a grudge, which she had taught me not to do. I knew too that Kirby understood me well enough to believe my sincerity in seeing my similarity in motive to the youth who had murdered. I trusted Kirby with my experience of forgiving, and she helped me make that experience an essential part of my life. I felt at peace.

Saying that I felt peace upon forgiving, though, isn't the same thing as saying that I didn't have pain over the loss or that I didn't grieve the hurt. In fact, the pain of the loss was probably the most significant pain I have ever felt in my life. The suddenness and the violence with which my mother was killed was a traumatic loss. I grieved. Talking with Kirby speeded the grief, strengthened my forgiveness, and prevented many doubts I might have had about whether I "really" had forgiven.

> *Saying that I felt peace upon forgiving, though, isn't the same thing as saying that I didn't have pain over the loss or that I didn't grieve the hurt.*

Analysis

Forgiveness is a complex, primarily emotional event. It's not just a change in the beliefs that we *should* forgive. Forgiveness doesn't make the crime less awful than we know it to be. It is not merely a change in attitude, or an act primarily of the will apart from our feelings.

> *Forgiveness doesn't make the crime less awful than we know it to be.*

I did not start that night willing to forgive. I started the night skeptically doubting the results of our own research, wondering if it was for me, wondering if our method really made a difference in the big hurts. The power of my emotions made me doubt research that I had poured thousands of hours of my life into. I wanted to put that research to the practical test, not as an intellectual exercise but as an act of emotional desperation to be able to deal with my overpowering emotions.

When I forgave from the heart, my emotions, including my thinking, bodily reactions, behavior, and feelings, were changed. I associated the traumatic scenes of harm, offense, and transgression with the healing scenes of empathy, humility, gratitude, and altruistic offering of a gift of forgiveness. But eventually I had to make my forgiveness more public.

When I forgave from the heart, my emotions, including my thinking, bodily reactions, behavior, and feelings, were changed.

Public forgiveness is not just acting in a forgiving way. It isn't simply saying that you've forgiven the perpetrator. It's not simply making a certificate or dropping a stone, or changing your behavior to be less vengeful.

Public forgiveness is like watching a hurricane approach. As the hurricane moves across the water and gains power, you see its power and destructiveness on television. You watch the Weather Channel, which draws a giant red triangle that extends from the eye of the hurricane to where it's expected to hit the United States. The hurricane moves closer hour by hour, day by day, and the red triangle remains fixed on the place where you live. Then, just as the storm is about to reach the shore, it stalls just off the coast, then turns north, swings out to sea, and dies, leaving a fresh, clear sky. It is nature's broom, sweeping away the pollution. Public forgiveness clears away the condemnation, criticism, and complaining. It leaves our conscience clean.

Sarah

Sarah had struggled to forgive the relatives who refused to support her during her time of financial strain. She worked through several self-help programs of forgiveness, saw a cleric for two sessions of counseling, and even went to twelve weeks of psychotherapy with a professional counselor. After each experience, she felt as if she had forgiven her relatives. But later, the pain of rejection would return and haunt her, until she found herself just as bitter, resentful, and hostile toward her relatives as she had been before. Sarah could forgive, but she could not hold on to her forgiveness. Then she attended one of our workshops on forgiveness, and near the end she received a revelation.

"Once forgiveness has been granted in one's heart and mind, it is always subject to doubt unless the commitment to forgive has been made public," said the workshop leader. Sarah constructed a Certificate of Forgiveness, which she displayed on her wall. When she doubted whether the forgiveness she had granted was real, she examined the Certificate of Forgiveness and reassured herself.

She also wrote a letter of forgiveness to each of her relatives. Even though she didn't send them because her relatives might have responded negatively, merely writing the letters made her forgiveness seem more real to her. Finally, she read the letters aloud to another member in the group. Hearing herself read the letters of forgiveness provided yet another piece of tangible evidence that she had indeed forgiven.

Apply What You've Learned

If you've practiced forgiving the four events you identified in Chapter 1, you have probably made some progress. By now, one or two might be fully forgiven. Perhaps your unforgiveness in the other two has lessened. It's time to consolidate your gains.

You know full well that you might still feel some of the remembered anger or fear, yet forgiveness eliminates the bitterness, resentment, hostility, and hatred. If you truly feel that you have forgiven, decide how to make a more public commitment of your forgiveness.

- Decondition yourself to the person by systematically recalling hurtful events without the attached emotion.
- Symbolize your forgiveness through using the First Stone, burning an account of the transgression, washing your hands of judgment, crossing out unforgiveness, or otherwise using a meaningful symbolic act.
- Write about your forgiveness in a certificate, letter, poem, song, or journal entry.
- Tell someone you trust, or at least say it out loud to yourself.

In the following chapter, we'll consider ways to hold on to the forgiveness you might have experienced.

CHAPTER 6

H: Hold On to Forgiveness

*Nothing great is created suddenly, any more than a
bunch of grapes or a fig. I answer you that there must be
time. Let it first blossom, then bear fruit, then ripen.*

—EPICTETUS

Even though Sarah, from the previous chapter, had created a
certificate stating how she forgave her relatives who did not
support her, she needed to take one more step. Sarah used another
bit of knowledge that helped her through the H step of the Pyramid Model to REACH Forgiveness—holding on to forgiveness.
When people have worked through the past to REACH Forgiveness, they often think (irrationally) that they will never remember
the hurt again. If they do recall the hurt and reexperience pain,
they often feel that their forgiveness was a fraud. Not so. For instance, consider Kindra.

Kindra had forgiven Ronnie a thousand times for the way he
betrayed their relationship. On their honeymoon, he had wanted
to rent motorbikes and see Nassau. Kindra said it was too dangerous. When Kindra developed a fever and diarrhea, Ronnie settled her in, then headed for the beach. At least that's what he said.

Instead, he headed for a motorbike rental shop, and took off on a jaunt.

He didn't see the car and the driver didn't see him. Ronnie slammed into the turning vehicle, and his head smacked the pavement. His traumatic head injury had been a constant source of friction between Kindra and Ronnie ever since. *It is so frustrating to live with someone with a brain injury,* Kindra thought for perhaps the thousandth time. *But what can I do?* Ronnie's moods were unpredictable. His memory was impaired. Sometimes he was just plain nasty to be around. Because he had always been so sweet before the injury, Kindra knew that Ronnie's injury was responsible for his changed personality. *The frustrating part is that he can't even remember going bike riding,* she thought.

Finally, she worked through forgiveness using the Pyramid Model to REACH Forgiveness. In the last step, she said aloud to the group she was attending that she had, this time, truly forgiven. The leader asked her to say it aloud individually to every person in the group. Her tears as she did so were relief valves of years of unforgiveness. Dealing with the frustration of Ronnie's problems would always bother her. Yet she knew that she would believe herself this time. She really had forgiven him.

Flashback to the Scene of the Murder

Two pools of blood stained the carpet in the house where I grew up. Even today, more than five years after the day I saw that blood, the mere thought of it triggers mental images that upset me. The two pools of blood on the carpet—one beneath the head and the other beneath the hips, each about the size of a dinner plate—are soaked into my memory. They trigger vile images that I am only partially successful at blocking. The blood splattered on the walls and door speaks of force and violence. I don't want to see them, but the images insist.

Over time, I flash back less often, but no less vividly. Each time I remember, I have to talk to myself about forgiveness, not listen to my chatter about my loss and pain. I had empathized with the youth who had murdered my mom and forgiven him. I had told the story of forgiveness often. But how do you keep forgiveness from slipping away when traumatic images keep forcing their way into consciousness? How do you maintain forgiveness when people ask searching questions about the trauma of the event? How do you hold on to forgiveness when thinking about a murderer who might be at large, terrorizing other people?

Simply knowing that hurt does not equal unforgiveness is important. To avoid being trapped once again in the Unforgiveness Loop, though, you must be active.

Holding On to Forgiveness Is Difficult

It's Simple—Simply Stop Those Thoughts

All we have to do is focus on stopping unwanted thoughts. Simple, right? Except for one tiny problem. It doesn't work.

All we have to do is focus on stopping unwanted thoughts. Simple, right? Except for one tiny problem. It doesn't work.

Daniel Wegner, a psychologist at the University of Virginia, has conducted research on how to stop unwanted thoughts. He has people try *not* to think about white bears.[1] You try it. Resolve in your mind that you will *not* remember the shape of the black nose, the shape of the bear, or the color of the fur. Resolve not to think of its paws. You are going to try as hard as you can for one minute not to think about a white bear. If you slip and think of the bear, tap the closed book with the palm of your hand, every time. Now, remember, *don't* think about white bears.

How did you do? If you are at all like me, you thought a lot about white bears. You may have even beaten the book to a pulp. (Is that where pulp fiction got its name?)

White bears climb into our minds. They crawl across the white walls in our office. They nose around the black shoe in the corner. They claw their way onto the tines of our fork. When we are actively trying to suppress a thought, everything seems to trigger it.

Perhaps you were successful at not thinking about white bears. If you were able to keep the bears at bay, it was probably because you filled your mind with something captivating. Maybe you thought about the plot of a recent movie. Maybe you tried to sing a popular song or visualize a music video. Perhaps you contemplated the intricate relationships among quantum physics, general relativity, and emerging complexity at the edge of chaos and order. (Well, different things distract different people.)

The point is, to keep from being mentally overrun with white bears, you must be active. Walter Mischel, another personality psychologist, placed children alone in a room with marshmallows and pretzels.[2] Mischel told each of them they could have two marshmallows if they waited until Mischel returned or they could have one pretzel if they couldn't wait. Regardless, they had to stay seated at the table. The forbidden marshmallows lay plumply in plain sight. The pretzel whispered saltily, "Eat me now. Put me out of my misery."

Mischel waited behind a one-way mirror, recording the children's behavior. Sometimes the kid had the pretzel in his or her mouth almost before Mischel got the camera rolling. Sometimes Mischel got fifteen minutes of tape before the child gave in.

Those children who waited distracted themselves vigorously. They sang. They looked around. They talked to themselves. Maybe they thought about nuclear physics. Who knows? One child even went to sleep.

Self-control takes effort. Social psychologist Roy Baumeister asked Case Western Reserve University students to skip lunch and arrive at his lab hungry.[3] Meanwhile he and his research assistants baked many chocolate chip cookies. Sweet smells wafted through the lab and filled the building. (Graduate students from bioengineering were reportedly walking across campus to beg for cookies.) When students who were research participants arrived, half were allowed to eat cookies. The others met a crueler fate.

Baumeister's associate asked the student's name. After consulting a list, the experimenter sadly announced, "Oh, I *am* sorry. You are in the radish condition." The radish condition? Surrounded by sights and smells of fresh chocolate chip cookies, those students had to eat a bowl of radishes. (It makes one wonder whether psychologists have a bit of a mean streak, doesn't it?)

Resisting the temptation to scarf up stray chocolate chip cookies (and perhaps do bodily injury to research scientists in the process) took its toll. Students who had to resist temptation exerted less self-control in a subsequent physical-exertion test. They were less willing to exert effort in a test of their grip strength.

Does Baumeister's study remind you of working out at a spa? Baumeister says that self-control is like a moral muscle. If we work hard to control ourselves on an important task, we might be at a disadvantage for controlling ourselves on another task in short order. It is like doing a set of sit-ups. If I max out, I cannot do as many sit-ups in a second set—unless I allow time for recovery.

Does that mean we shouldn't practice self-control? Baumeister found that students who practiced regular self-control on one task—such as attending to posture, flossing daily, or trying to think nice things about people—did better on other tests of self-control. Like a moral muscle, self-control gets stronger as we use it, but two back-to-back tests might fatigue the moral muscle.

Practicing forgiveness whenever we recall the transgression is an act of self-control. Look back at Figure 5.1. When we forgive, we disconnect the Unforgiveness Loop from the Transgression Loop, and we connect a Forgiveness Loop to the Transgression. That act is an exercise of self-control. If we ruminate again, we can undo our hard work.

Even after we have forgiven, it is not easy to resist unforgiveness. For many people, unforgiveness is the low point into which they automatically roll if left alone. Holding on to forgiveness requires an uphill fight.

Six Actions You Can Take to Hold On to Forgiveness

There are six things you can do to hold on to forgiveness. *One: Realize that the pain of a remembered hurt is not unforgiveness.* Remind yourself that feeling the pain associated with remembering a hurt is not the same thing as feeling unforgiveness. Unforgiveness requires rumination. Don't give in to vengeful rumination.

Two: Don't dwell on negative emotions. It's natural to feel emotions when you recall being hurt. You could reexperience anger or fear in a milder form. But if you don't dwell on the emotions, then unforgiveness won't regrow. Actively distract yourself rather than instructing yourself not to dwell on the emotions. Remember Daniel Wegner's white bears.

Three: Remind yourself that you have forgiven the person. Recall the times when you talked to a trusted friend or partner about having forgiven the person. Remember that you have said aloud that you have forgiven. Say it aloud to yourself in privacy.

Four: Seek reassurance from a partner or friend. You might have talked with a partner or friend about having forgiven the person. Your partner or friend should be able to remind you of that.

Five: Use the documents that you created. Read your forgiveness certificate. Read the letter that you wrote describing your forgiveness.

Six: Look at the Pyramid Model to REACH Forgiveness (Figure 1.3) *and think through the steps again.* If you simply don't believe that you have completely forgiven, maybe you haven't. Trust your feelings if they persist. Perhaps there are actually things you haven't forgiven even though there are many things you have. Work through the REACH steps with other transgressions. This will help you deal with whatever might still be unforgiven.

> *If you simply don't believe that you have completely forgiven, maybe you haven't. Trust your feelings if they persist.*

Becoming a more forgiving person will not spring suddenly into existence. It will grow like fruit in your life if the plant from which it is to grow is nurtured.

> *Becoming a more forgiving person will not spring suddenly into existence. It will grow like fruit in your life if the plant from which it is to grow is nurtured.*

Can Unforgiveness Be a Character Disposition?

In Clint Eastwood's Academy Award–winning movie *Unforgiven,* Eastwood plays a retired gunfighter named Will Munny. The Schofield Kid, an itinerant young gunfighter, comes by Will's farm to see if Will will join him in collecting a bounty. Two cowboys in Big Whiskey, Montana, cut the face of a prostitute in the town, and the prostitute's friends collected money to offer a bounty to have the two men killed. So the Schofield Kid attempts to persuade Will to seek part of the bounty with him.

Will claims he has changed. He has given up gunfighting and bounty chasing. He is doing his best to rear his children after his wife died. He is responsibly eking out a living farming the hard ground of Kansas. He turns down the Schofield Kid and refuses to seek the bounty.

After the Kid leaves, though, Will changes his mind. Will tries to get back in the saddle to seek the bounty, but he keeps falling off his horse. It isn't easy, but eventually he fights his way back into his lifestyle of hate and violence.

Will and the Schofield Kid are joined by a friend, Ned. They ride together to Big Whiskey. Will shoots one of the perpetrators in the stomach. It takes him a long time to die. Ned leaves and heads back to Kansas, having no stomach for bounty hunting.

The next morning the Schofield Kid kills the second perpetrator. Later, as they discuss the Kid's murder of the outlaw, the Kid admits that the killing is his first. He vows to head home.

A prostitute arrives with the money for the bounty. She also brings news that Will's friend Ned was captured by the sheriff and died under interrogation.

Will is outraged. He begins to drink heavily to numb himself to what he is about to do. Will vows to exact vengeance on the town for Ned's murder. Loaded with bullets and booze, he heads into Big Whiskey.

Will enters the saloon and shoots the sheriff and five men. The sheriff, while dying, says to Will, "I don't deserve this."

"Nobody does," says Will, who shoots the sheriff again. As Will rides out of town, he yells, "You give my friend a decent burial, you hear. Or I'll come back and kill you all."

Unforgiven is not just a shoot-'em-up Western. It is a serious movie about people's character. In that movie, virtually everyone seems to be unforgiving, unforgiven, and unredeemable. The movie raises questions about whether unforgiveness is a terminal character trait that is endemic to humanity.

Although an act of hurt and offense (hearing that Ned had been tortured to death) enraged Will, the movie asks whether that event or other horrid circumstances make people unforgiving, or whether Will or people in general are unforgiving at the core and are simply waiting for an event to justify vengeful violence. The fact is that for twelve years Will had been responsible and self-controlled. Was that period a thin veneer of civility due to the positive restraint of his wife and children? Was he so unforgiving at heart that with the slightest motivation and provocation, he chucked aside the self-restraint of a virtuous life and resumed his (true) unforgiving ways?

On the other hand, perhaps humans are at root forgiving and peace-loving. After all, Will was the soul of peace for twelve years. Ned refused to participate in violence. The Kid was morally sickened by having murdered. An endnote to the movie says that Will later resumed his peaceful life.

Are people *by nature* unforgiving or forgiving? Our answer probably resides more in our preference for theology or philosophy than in facts and evidence. People will probably never agree. We can agree, though, that people develop long-lasting dispositions that persist for years.

Some people are characterized by a disposition of unforgivingness. Across time and situations they seem habitually unforgiving. Anger is never far beneath the surface. Fear of hurt or offense lurks within their psyche. They have been wounded so deeply or so often, or have ruminated so much, that they seem to have radar for rejection. They are targets waiting expectantly for the arrows of offense to prick them in sensitive spots. Resentment and bitterness sharpen their tone of voice to an aggrieved whine.

I recently talked with such a friend. I'll call her Janet. I hadn't seen her for perhaps twelve years. She dropped by my office after work with her husband and two children.

"Have you been in town long?" I asked.

"Nah," she said. "We had to come by to sign papers on some rental property we just sold. Besides, I really didn't want to see any of the old gang."

"Why not?"

"I've fallen out of contact with most of 'em. Myra—you remember her, don't you?—wrote me for a few years, but even she stopped writing. I have no use for any of them."

"What about Emma?" I knew that she and Emma had been best friends when they attended school.

"We had a falling-out. I gave and gave to her when we roomed together. Then, right before we graduated, I asked her to run a simple errand for me. She refused! Her boyfriend was coming to town, and she was afraid that he wouldn't want to spend the couple of hours it might take to drive down to Williamsburg and back. Once she unfurled her true colors, I saw that she didn't really care about me."

"That's too bad. I know you were good friends."

"No big loss. I cared more than she did."

Janet chatted awhile longer. Then, with a final sarcastic comment, she and her husband left to sign the papers on the rental property.

CAN WE HAVE A CHARACTER THAT IS BOTH UNFORGIVING AND FORGIVING?

Some people with unforgiving characters also have forgiving characters. They seem to get hurt easily. They seem sensitive and reactive. They ruminate about hurts and develop strong grudges. They are unforgiving of almost every transgression. They have an unforgiving character.

After a while, though, they forgive almost every transgression. The same sensitivity that makes them prone to grudges makes them emotional and fervent forgivers. They have a forgiving character. While they have a perpetual backlog of grudges, the grudges always seem to be a fresh crop.

Most of us seem to gravitate more to one character than the other. We can lean toward bitterness (and be bitterly unforgiving of ourselves for our bitterness). Or we can lean toward forgiveness.

WHAT KIND OF CHARACTER DO YOU WANT TO HAVE?

Few people aspire to be unforgiven and unforgiving, like Will Munny. Instead, we want to be like Jean Valjean in Victor Hugo's novel *Les Misérables*. Valjean stole some silverware from Monsignor Bienvenue, a church official who had provided food and shelter for a destitute Valjean.

Early the next morning, Valjean was apprehended and faced certain prison. In front of the accusing police, the monsignor said,

"My friend, you forgot the silver candlesticks that I said you could have."

When the police left, a grateful Valjean tried to return the silverware and candlesticks, but the monsignor was in earnest about the gifts. Valjean fell to his knees in front of the monsignor, a forgiven and, from that moment, forgiving man.

In the Broadway play based on the novel, Javert (Valjean's nemesis) had earlier sung, "A man like you can never change." But Valjean did change. Javert, on the other hand, was an unchanging hound of justice. He refused to change, and one day it drove him to drown himself.

Did Will Munny change? He was a bounty hunter, then a family man, then a bounty hunter. I believe people can change. Long ago I heard a brief poem:

> *Two natures beat within my breast.*
> *One is cursed, and one is blessed.*
> *One I love, and one I hate.*
> *The one I feed will dominate.*
>
> —Anonymous

We each have within us Valjean and Javert. We have a need for justice and a need for forgiveness. Either can get out of balance. The virtue of the love of justice can easily turn to pursuit of revenge. Forgiveness is more difficult to corrupt, but it can become a disdain for justice in extreme cases. For most of us, though, we forgive too little rather than too much.

We each have within us Valjean and Javert. We have a need for justice and a need for forgiveness. Either can get out of balance.

Ten Steps to Becoming a More Forgiving Person

I have described below ten steps that you might take over a period of time to help you become a more forgiving person. If you apply these steps, you'll have a challenge that can occupy you for many years. I believe it is a challenge worthy of a lifetime.

STEP ONE: IDENTIFY YOUR GREATEST WOUNDS FROM THE PAST

To be a more forgiving person, you must forgive more future and past wounds. You cannot predict which wounds will arise. Those will be your character tests. Try to remember wounds from your past and try to forgive them. Refer to the hurts you recalled at the end of Chapter 1. That is a start. Add to your list.

STEP TWO: FORGIVE ONE WOUND AT A TIME

We can change our motives—like Jean Valjean—and decide we want to be more forgiving in the future. But to forgive, we must tackle hurts one at a time.

For each event, work carefully through the Pyramid Model to REACH Forgiveness. As you forgive, check off your events to show yourself that you're making progress. Don't feel that you must forgive perfectly. Move toward forgiving along a broad front.

STEP THREE: IDENTIFY HEROES OF FORGIVENESS

Our heroes can act as models who inspire us to forgive. With the cynicism of the 1960s, 1970s, and 1980s, people rarely identified their heroes. My generation and those following did not often teach that there were heroes. Today, few people have heroes.

Whom do you want to be like? Examine your experience and

Ten Steps to Becoming a More Forgiving Person

1. Identify your greatest wounds from the past.

2. Forgive one wound at a time.

3. Identify heroes of forgiveness.

4. Examine yourself.

5. Reduce negative traits, cultivate virtue.

6. Change your experience of the past.

7. Plan your self-improvement strategy.

8. Practice forgiving under imagined conditions.

9. Practice forgiving day to day.

10. Seek help from someone you trust.

---

determine whether there are people you admire. Why? Do they seem to forgive quickly and easily? Here are some of my heroes.

Eric Liddell came to most people's attention as a result of the movie *Chariots of Fire.* The movie dramatized Liddell's moral stance toward the British Olympic authorities, but that event was merely one in a virtuous life. After the games, Liddell went to China as a missionary. When World War II broke out, almost twenty years after the Olympic Games that were dramatized in *Chariots of Fire,* Liddell was imprisoned. In a prison camp, he consistently gave up his food to help other prisoners stay alive. He stood up for his faith. He forgave the people who abused him and other prisoners. Eventually, Liddell died in that prison camp. His life was a testimony to love and forgiveness.

Another paragon of forgiveness is Aleksandr Solzhenitsyn. Solzhenitsyn spent much of his adult life in the Russian gulag, the Soviet prison-camp system. Despite his suffering, when he was released, he wrote with compassion, empathy, and understanding about the people who had imprisoned him. Nonetheless, he was firm in decrying the system that imprisoned people. Solzhenitsyn was the perfect blend of justice and forgiveness.

Mohandas Gandhi was firm in his resolve to conquer prejudice and oppressive treatment within his native India through nonviolent protest. Despite being the object of violence numerous times, Gandhi persistently forgave. His was a blend of nonviolent social justice and forgiveness.

Jesus of Nazareth is the cornerstone of Christianity, which is built on forgiveness. The central narrative of Christianity is that Jesus gave his life to take the sin of all people, who were sinners against God and other humans. Justice demanded death as payment for sin. Jesus voluntarily took the punishment. God granted forgiveness. In his life on earth, Jesus was abused, persecuted, and finally tortured. Yet as his life drew to an end, he prayed that God would forgive those who did evil against him, which showed his own forgiving heart toward those people.

It is helpful to measure your life against your models of forgiveness. Your ideal might be religious, a historical hero, a contemporary hero (such as Nelson Mandela or Desmond Tutu), a public figure who seems forgiving (such as Oprah Winfrey, Bill Cosby, or Diane Sawyer), or a person you have known who is an excellent forgiver. Setting your sights upward on a model lifts your head. It focuses you on others, not yourself.

In measuring your life against a model, though, don't fall into a shame trap. We all fall short of our ideals. We all feel guilty because our lives lack virtue. I hope that looking to models of forgiveness will motivate you to live a more virtuous life, not shame you into self-condemnation.

In measuring your life against a model, though, don't fall into a shame trap.

STEP FOUR: EXAMINE YOURSELF

If you're like me, it's sobering to see how many unforgiven events clog up my free flow of love. Although I forgave the murderer, I have seen repeatedly, not just that first night, how often I do the very things I have vowed not to do. Novelist Frank Peretti wrote an unforgettable book called *The Oath*. In that book, a dark, gooey stain oozed from the hearts of those who practiced evil. As evil became etched into a person's character, the stain spread from the invisible heart to the visible chest and clothes. Sooner or later, the person infected with the stain would embrace evil and be devoured by a beast. Unforgiveness is like that dark stain. Once it gets a beachhead, it spreads.

Practicing unforgiveness is a trap. We start out thinking it's a safe place to be, and we worm our way inside inch by inch. We pass sharp wires that face the center of the trap. Once we're inside, practicing habitual unforgiveness, we don't want to go back. To forgive, we must face the jabs of making restitution and the stabs of trying to change our character. We can wallow miserably in guilt and self-condemnation. Or we can face the jabs.

The good news is this. When we meet unforgiveness head on and forgive, we start a character reaction—like a chemical reaction that titrates the dark stain of unforgiveness. When we practice forgiveness, we can be "trapped" by empathy, compassion, and a heart full of love and mercy.

If you wish to become a more forgiving person, examine yourself. Be (first) honest and (second) gentle with yourself. Ironically, when unforgiveness of others is a habit, it's easy to turn the same condemnation on yourself.

> *If you wish to become a more forgiving person, examine yourself. Be (first) honest and (second) gentle with yourself. Ironically, when unforgiveness of others is a habit, it's easy to turn the same condemnation on yourself.*

Some people tend to be ruminators. They think, worry, and stew over events. Others seem to let troubles roll off them. They are called dissipators. Ruminators tend to experience more depression, anxiety, fear, and hostility than do dissipators. Ruminators are more often unforgiving.

That doesn't mean that dissipators are immune to unforgiveness. While they may not stew about transgressions, the stain of unforgiveness can be just as wide, just as messy.

The flip side means that ruminators are often more aware of their struggles than are dissipators. So they are often primed to do something about their unforgiveness. They tend to ponder empathically more than do dissipators.

After my mother's murder, I experienced forgiveness that helped heal my trauma. Even better, though, my self-examination helped me to become aware that I needed a "heart transplant." I found that unforgiveness was more of a struggle for me than I ever thought it could be. So, as Solzhenitsyn in the gulag was able to say, "Thank you prison camp for bringing this illumination into my life, which otherwise I would have lost." I can then thank God because out of the evil of my mother's murder God has brought good from it. I could honestly say to my mother's murderer, like the Jewish patriarch Joseph said to his brothers, "You meant it for evil but God has brought from it good" (Gen. 50:20).

Perhaps you want to examine your life. How unforgiving are you in general as a person? How forgiving? If you aren't particularly unforgiving, is that because you forgive quickly or because you simply haven't developed much unforgiveness?

STEP FIVE: REDUCE NEGATIVE TRAITS, CULTIVATE VIRTUE

My self-examination has motivated me to try to replace my unforgiving with virtue. I don't always succeed. Still, I try to practice love, mercy, empathy, sympathy, and compassion. Those are at the core of forgiveness.

By examining my life, I concluded that I wanted to develop a more virtuous character. You might decide the same. Write a list of personal qualities that you would like to increase. Your list might differ from mine. For each trait, complete this sentence: "If I were more _____, I would _____ more often." Fill in the first blank with a personal quality and the second blank with specific behaviors. For instance, "If I were more loving toward people at work, I would compliment them, try to understand them, empathize with them, and forgive them more often." Determine which traits are most important. Plan specific steps to do those behaviors.

Don't phrase your goals in negative terms. For example, do *not* say, "If I were more loving toward people at work, I would not criticize more often." Instead of saying what you would *not* do, say what you *would* do. If you follow these steps, you have begun a program to help yourself become more virtuous. It is my hope that being more forgiving is one of your goals.

Step Six: Change Your Experience of the Past

If you think you're too unforgiving, you didn't become that way this morning. Freud said, "The child is father to the man." Wounds in your past may have started you along the road that led to frequent unforgiveness.

While I cannot change what actually happened, I can certainly change:

- My perception of what happened
- My emotional and mental associations of what happened
- My understanding of the meaning of the event

When you empathize with the person who hurt you, you are adding information that you had not previously perceived. When you recall in humility that you might have provoked your friend, you are changing your perception. When you experience a strong sense of empathy, you change the mental and emotional associations with the event. When you feel guilt over your role in a misunderstanding and gratitude over having been forgiven, you change your mental and emotional associations.

When you set a goal for yourself of wanting to have a forgiving character (Step Five) and you see unforgiveness as working against that goal, you can change the meaning of acts of revenge or retaliation. When you do forgive, you can see that your forgiveness is more than an isolated event. It is another block in a structure of virtue.

You can also use your imagination to change your experience of the past. Imagine yourself in some setting in which you're going to face the person who wounded you. Now imagine that one of your heroes of forgiveness is there with you (see Step Three). Perhaps it is your mother. Perhaps it is a favorite teacher. Perhaps it is Jesus or Gandhi. Imagine facing your nemesis and talking about the painful wounds of the past while being encouraged by your hero of forgiveness. Vividly imagine the scene as if it were really happening.

> *Imagine facing your nemesis and talking about the painful wounds of the past while being encouraged by your hero of forgiveness.*

You can literally change your experience of the past by such vivid imagery. Memory experts tell us that memory is literally rebuilt each time you call it to consciousness. When you recall past wounds but change things in your mind's eye, you rebuild a more positive past for yourself.

STEP SEVEN: PLAN YOUR SELF-IMPROVEMENT STRATEGY

If you fall short of your ideal, decide to do something about it. Take one step at a time. As Lao-tzu said, "A journey of a thousand miles begins with a single step." Your self-improvement strategy might involve doing more honest self-evaluation, reading inspirational books, or developing a more sincere life of faith. Depending on your experiences, you will design a strategy that aims you toward being a more forgiving person.

As I have thought and written about forgiving, I've been challenged by my own failures to forgive. It has damaged my self-esteem. But I have found that to be a good thing rather than a bad thing. It motivated me to lay aside pride and pursue virtue.

Step Eight: Practice Forgiving Under Imagined Conditions

To forgive, continually practice forgiveness. Select one of the past events that you have not forgiven. Perhaps this involves a person with whom you often talk. (You will benefit the most if you go back to Chapter 1 and select a specific transgression that you are still trying to forgive.)

Set aside ten minutes to imagine discussing the event in which the person hurt you. Do this three times. First, imagine that the conversation worked perfectly to produce forgiveness. Imagine this thoroughly. That is what in psychology is called using yourself as a mastery model.

Of course, life is rarely perfect. After you have completed your mastery imagery, imagine the same scene again. This time, assume that the person provoked you. Imagine how you might respond if you were a perfectly forgiving person. Conclude the scene by again imagining that your conversation led to forgiving. Imagine this now.

Imagine your conversation a third time. This time, imagine that you tried to talk about being hurt, got angry, and said something you knew you would regret. See yourself apologizing immediately. Change directions and get the conversation back on a positive track.

If you can imagine yourself under these three conditions— mastery, having been provoked, and having lost your temper—you have covered much of the waterfront. By rehearsing, you can make it more likely that you will live out a forgiving character in real life.

STEP NINE: PRACTICE FORGIVING DAY TO DAY

The tests of whether you are developing a more forgiving character will come in how you respond to daily real-life provocations. Perhaps you had a recent conflict with your spouse. Maybe your child acted rebelliously. Maybe you were criticized by a coworker or an unreasonable employer. Prepare yourself for the possible challenges you will face in dealing with this person each day. Think about how you might be provoked and imagine yourself forgiving. Then gird yourself for the battle of living out your forgiveness.

STEP TEN: SEEK HELP FROM SOMEONE YOU TRUST

What if you're still unable to forgive? If the unforgiveness emotionally upsets you, then you might want to seek help from someone who can be objective and help you forgive more.

Friends provide emotional support, but often they're so supportive that they cannot help you move past your current unforgiveness. If you say, "I *want* to forgive him," a loyal friend might respond, "I've seen the way he treats you, and it's shameful." Such statements emotionally support you but also keep you stuck in the rut of unforgiveness.

Like friends, your spouse can help you work through your unforgiveness and develop a more forgiving character. Your spouse often knows more sides of you than do your friends. He or she has often seen more of the negative parts of your character. Yet, under the best circumstances, your spouse is committed to remaining in a loving relationship with you and is often more capable of being honest and loving at the same time. Of course, not all marriages exist under the best circumstances.

A professional helper, such as a clergyperson, counselor, or therapist, is trained to be the most objective. He or she can help you examine your relationships without the investment of needing to live with you.

Applying the Pyramid Model to REACH Forgiveness

A woman—let's call her Susan—has been unforgiving toward her father for fifteen years. Their relationship was completely severed after Susan's mother's untimely death by cancer four years ago. Susan felt that she had no reason ever to go home again.

Then she learned that her father had prostate cancer. Susan decided that she should try to reconcile with him. She knew she had to forgive him first.

Susan's father always seemed to be at work. He was available to everyone but his only daughter. When he was at home, he was often gruff. He never seemed to understand her. The event that stuck out in her mind was as vivid as if it had happened yesterday.

Susan began to employ the Pyramid Model to REACH Forgiveness. She vividly recalled a hurt (R). As a teenager, Susan had been looking forward to her first prom. Asked as a sophomore, she was the envy of her friends. The week before the prom, she stayed out with her friends, drinking sodas and eating ice cream at the local Friendly's. They were having a great time. Suddenly, in horror, she looked up and saw her father striding toward her. It was almost an hour past her curfew. Susan was mortified as her father dragged her by the arm from the restaurant. The next day he forbade her to attend the prom.

To empathize (E) with her father at first seemed beyond her capacity, but she was determined to try to forgive. She began to imagine, tentatively at first, what her father might have felt as he and her mother waited at home for her. Tidbits of his angry speech flooded back into her memory. "We were worried sick. We know that Jennifer [Susan's friend] isn't an experienced driver, and we were afraid something might have happened." Susan imagined the fear that must have passed between her father and mother. Her mother, she remembered, always seemed to magnify mounds into mountains. Her father always said that her mother's catastrophizing drove him crazy. Susan fell asleep having a sense of sympathy for him.

It was two days later when Susan had time to reflect on forgiving again. As Susan began to see things from her father's point of view, she had to admit to herself that she had "pushed the envelope" when it came to limits. She frustrated her parents by her rebellious attitude. Although Susan still believed that her father's insensitivity was inexcusable, she could see how she had provoked him. She realized he had his own set of pressures. She had moved from sympathizing to empathizing with her father. Her empathic understanding did not make his inexcusable behavior *right*. But it made it more understandable. Understanding, she wanted to forgive.

Susan began to employ the third step, the altruistic gift of forgiveness (A). She recalled several times in her youth when her mother and father had forgiven her. She thought carefully about each incident, but it didn't seem to further her forgiveness. She couldn't seem to get immersed in any of those memories.

The next day, she recalled an incident that had occurred the week before. Susan had offended her boss. Even though the consequences could have been disastrous, her boss dismissed the incident. "No problem," he said, waving his hand. "All is forgiven." Susan left her boss's office with a smile and a light step. It was easy to see how forgiving her father might free him in the same way.

For two days, she turned all these memories over in her mind. She knew she should forgive. But she had lived with resentment for fifteen years. It was hard to let go.

It was a video she saw that weekend that pushed her over the edge into forgiveness. Ironically, the movie was a forgettable crime thriller about revenge. After the movie, she lay in bed, rethinking the prom episode. She forgave her father.

Unable to contain herself, she phoned her best friend, Gina, and poured out her experience of finally forgiving her father. "Forgiveness is like drinking hot coffee after being out in the snow for three hours of cross-country skiing," said Susan. "My legs are tired. My feet and toes are cold. My fingers feel as if they are going to fall off. Then I grasp a warm cup of coffee, inhale deeply to breathe in the aroma of coffee and the steam, and feel the warmth of the first gulp of liquid spread out through my entire torso. That's the way I felt when I forgave Dad—flooded with warmth." As Susan and Gina chatted, Susan was practicing the fourth step of the Pyramid Model to REACH Forgiveness, committing publicly to forgive (C).

When she put down the phone, she thought about phoning her father even though she knew he didn't keep the same late-night hours that she and Gina kept. As she thought of calling, some of the hurt came back. Old feelings of shame, embarrassment, fear, and sadness welled up within her. *I assumed that if I forgave him, I'd be finished with those feelings,* she thought. Then she remembered: *Hurt isn't the same thing as unforgiveness. I can accept the reality that my father's actions were truly hurtful, but my unforgiveness is gone as long as I don't dwell on the negative.* By understanding the fundamental difference between remembered hurts and unforgiveness, Susan was practicing the fifth step, holding on to forgiveness (H).

Susan intentionally used the Pyramid Model to REACH Forgiveness. Her forgiveness took place over a period of several days. That's not always the case. Sometimes it happens quickly, even with events that are very traumatic, such as my mother's murder. Sometimes forgiveness happens only after empathizing for hours repeatedly and attempting to forgive for days or weeks. Over the years I have become convinced that there are no easy answers or glib formulas for how to forgive. The Pyramid Model to REACH Forgiveness provides five steps, but don't be disappointed if you employ the steps and unforgiveness does not suddenly disappear. Keep repeating the steps. Forgiveness might soon break through.

Forgiveness and the Transformation of Relationships

Forgiving my mother's murderer was a one-time event. The chances are low that I will ever have to forgive the murderer again simply because I don't know for sure who he is, and even if I did, I wouldn't regularly interact with him.

Most of the time when we struggle to forgive, it's because a person hurts us repeatedly. When that happens, we usually change our tune from talking of specific transgressions and go from saying "I can't forgive that" to "I can't forgive *him!*" We generalize. Many transgressions coalesce into a person.

When we see the person, stress increases. We feel angry. We are bitter. Hatred flares up like a signal flare, alerting us to potential danger. How can we possibly forgive the person? *Forgiving everything he has done to me,* we think, *could take a lifetime.*

Nonetheless, the road to forgiving a person winds its way through forgiving important (symbolic) events that remind you of why you cannot forgive. Work through the Pyramid Model to

REACH Forgiveness for each event that comes to symbolize the person's blameworthy character. Once you forgive those symbolic events, you may find that your animosity has evaporated.

In the first part of this book, you have learned a five-step method to help you REACH forgiveness. You have practiced each step. You saw how to use the method to help yourself develop a more forgiving character. You saw how to pick symbolic hurts to forgive a hard-to-forgive person.

In each case, we assumed that the person you are trying to forgive isn't present. When you have to deal with the person, life becomes more complicated. Now the person can respond to what you do. He or she has his or her own agenda and perspective on the events. The person might believe that *you* are at fault. He or she might hurt you again.

We need to take the next step and consider how our interactions can help or hinder forgiving. Rebuilding trust is the context of seeking, granting, and accepting forgiveness. That is the focus of the second part of this book.

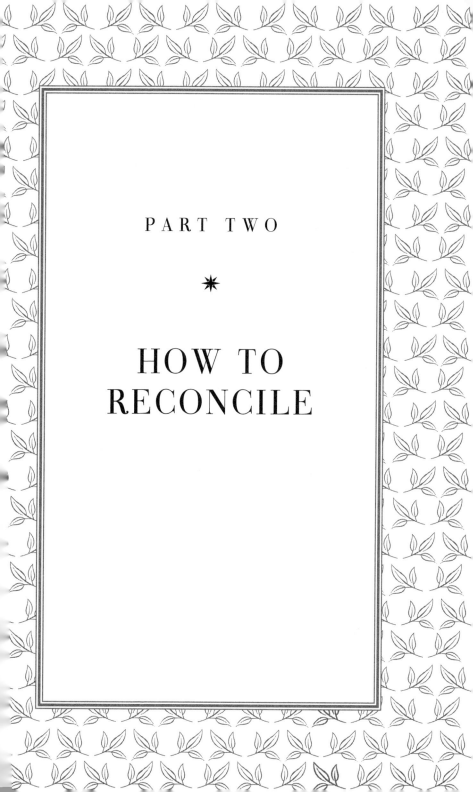

PART TWO

*

HOW TO
RECONCILE

CHAPTER 7

Decisions

You cannot build a bridge by starting in the middle.
Bridge-builders begin from the side they are on.
— JOHN PAUL LEDERAC

In our laboratory and clinic, after I had developed the Pyramid Model to REACH Forgiveness, my students and I began to apply it. Jennifer Ripley helped groups of couples from Richmond who were seeking marital enrichment. Near the end of the group, we had partners talk to each other about past unforgiven transgressions. Imagine the scene. Five couples were scattered around a room. One group leader tried to monitor those separate conversations about past hurts. When the group leader was nearby, most couples talked calmly. But the group leader always had his or her back to several couples. Voices began to rise. The group leader would drift toward the rising voices. Under the leader's attention, the partners would calm back down. Meanwhile, though, two other arguments would erupt. The group leader was like a pinball, moving back and forth among five couples, but no group leader could control five conversations. Some wounds were healed, but some old wounds surfaced. We had not taught partners how to talk about the transgression itself. Some talked harshly with each other. They sometimes hurt each other anew.

By looking hard at our study's weaknesses, Jennifer and I saw ways to correct them. The scientific method had worked. We had new ideas. We just hope those first groups of couples forgave us.

We realized that forgiving was more complex when people had to go nose to nose with another person than when individuals forgive an absent person. (This might seem like a "duh" insight, but we hadn't taken it seriously prior to Jennifer's study.)

We began to think about forgiveness within the context of reconciliation.[1] In this part of the book, I describe how to forgive when you are still in a relationship with someone who hurt you. I also describe how people can reconcile. As with forgiving, empathy is the core of reconciling.

Differences Between Forgiveness and Reconciliation

An Added Dimension

People can forgive a person who is absent, such as a parent who has been long dead. They can also learn to forgive someone they must face daily. When you have to interact with someone, two roads open up. Discussing hurts can resolve or dissolve the relationship.

The other person can talk back, bring up times you inflicted hurt, push your buttons, and provoke you to blind rage. But the other person can also be accommodating, contrite, remorseful, and loving. How you both interact will determine the future of the relationship. Will you tick each other off or tackle the problem? Will you jerk each other's chain or chain your hearts closer together?

> *How you both interact will determine the future of the relationship. Will you tick each other off or tackle the problem? Will you jerk each other's chain or chain your hearts closer together?*

WHAT'S THE DIFFERENCE BETWEEN FORGIVING AND RECONCILING?

When people interact, we are no longer considering mere forgiveness. We are talking reconciliation. *Reconciliation is restoring trust in a relationship in which trust has been damaged.* Reconciliation requires both people to be trustworthy.

> *Reconciliation is restoring trust in a relationship in which trust has been damaged.*

Forgiveness and reconciliation are often confused with each other (Table 7.1). Forgiveness is internal. I replace negative emotions. I grant forgiveness as a gift. Reconciliation is interpersonal. It is not granted, but earned. It occurs within our relationship.

Reconciliation and forgiveness are related to each other but are not joined at the hip. We can forgive and not reconcile. For instance, I can forgive my father for ways he transgressed against me when he was alive. Yet we cannot reconcile because he is dead.

> *Reconciliation and forgiveness are related to each other but are not joined at the hip.*

TABLE 7.1

A Quick Comparison of Forgiveness and Reconciliation

	FORGIVENESS	RECONCILIATION
Who?	One person	Two or more people
What?	Gift granted	Earned, not granted
How?	Emotional replacement	Behavioral replacement
Where?	Within your body	Within your relationship
How to?	Pyramid Model to REACH Forgiveness	Bridge to Reconciliation

We can reconcile and not forgive. Think of all those office squabbles. If we had to go to the mat and explicitly forgive every small breach of trust, we would never get any work done. We would spend many days tromping up and down the Pyramid. Yet because we must work together, we find ways to rebuild trust.

FEELING FORGIVENESS CAN MOTIVATE RECONCILIATION

Even though forgiveness and reconciliation aren't joined, they are clearly related. When we forgive, we are often moved to pursue reconciliation. Let me go back to shortly after my mother's death for an illustration.

After I returned from Tennessee and my mother's funeral, I talked about my feelings only to my family. I was emotional whenever the subject of her death came up, so I tried not to talk about the murder. I passed along the basic information to my friends and colleagues and accepted their gracious condolence. Then I changed the topic fast.

Only with Kirby could I really let my hair down. I could talk safely about the pain that I felt. We spent many hours on long walks—her listening, me trying to make sense of the murder. How did it fit into my world? What would it mean not to have Mama alive?

Almost four full months after the murder, I spoke about it publicly for the first time. I was to receive an award for teaching. I was slated to speak to about five hundred students, parents, and university faculty.

I talked about the noble privilege of the teacher. "Character," I said, "is often more difficult to develop and to maintain than is an inquiring mind. As teachers, we have the noble yet often humbling task of helping students develop positive character traits." I talked of how my own character had been tested by the death of my mother. For the first time, I described publicly what her murder scene was like. I shared from the heart how I reacted—first with rage, then with the lust for murder, and finally with peaceful forgiveness of the murderer. I concluded, "Life often throws a sudden test of character before us. Will our students—and will we, as students of life—be able to pass our tests of character?"

At the end of the night's award program, at least fifteen people moved forward and shook my hand. Most shared their own struggles at forgiving people. Several made a passionate vow to find the person who had hurt or offended them to make things right—to reconcile.

I was amazed. I had hoped to help teachers want to teach positive values. Yet the effects of sharing that I could forgive my mom's murderer extended far beyond my hoped-for effect on teachers. Teachers, parents, students, and administrators were moved to try once again to enter into the difficult task of forgiving those whom they had tried to forgive many times before. Even more, several wanted to reconcile with those who had hurt them. They wanted to restore their friendship. Hearing about forgiveness had unleashed a desire in them to restore trust in a trust-scarred relationship.

Encouraged, a month later I talked once again about forgiving the murderer. That time I was speaking to a conference of professional counselors. At the end of that talk, people once again moved forward and shared their personal struggles and stories of forgiveness. They wanted to know how I forgave. They wanted to test their character with a challenge to forgive. As before, knowing that I could forgive a tragic murder helped them want to make things right with people they had hurt and with those who had hurt them.

Yet sometimes, despite a desire on each side to reconcile, the trust gap widens like the earth opening up during an earthquake. An innocent remark ignites an explosion. A not-so-innocent gibe triggers an angry fire that had been smoldering beneath the surface. Talking about forgiveness and seeking to reconcile are risky. We have all tried to reconcile with people only to have the conversation blow up in our face. If only there were a foolproof way to restore trust.

How Can People Reconcile?

When we have invested our time and much of our life in a relationship, we usually want to reconcile. But how? The emotional terrain seems littered with nasty hidden mines that spring up and cut you off at the knees or blow your head off. Sometimes it seems easier just to avoid the other person than to step out in an attempt to reconcile.

I began to study reconciliation.[2] To my surprise, I uncovered many fields of study, which included primatology (how non-human primates repair conflict),[3] child-child conflict, restorative justice, international conflict negotiations, political reconciliation, and religious dialogues. Quite a diverse set of bedfellows!

From these very different fields, we began to discern common principles. Like chemists, we spun the elements, distilled them, and purified them into four steps. These make up the Bridge to Reconciliation.

The Bridge to Reconciliation

To build the Bridge to Reconciliation (Figure 7.1), each person offers four planks to join together, motivated by a mutual desire to make the relationship better rather than let it unravel. Both partners may try to reconcile but be skeptical about the outcome. But if they want to save the relationship, they at least need to make an honest try at reconciliation. The trust gap cannot be leaped. It must be bridged. A bridge does not spontaneously appear; it must be built. As John Paul Lederac, peace worker in many foreign countries, was quoted at the beginning of this chapter, "You cannot build a bridge by starting in the middle. Bridge-builders begin from the side they are on."

The Bridge to Reconciliation is my way of helping two people build a bridge across the trust gap. Using the principles I described in the Pyramid Model to REACH Forgiveness, the Bridge to Reconciliation adds principles about how to reconcile that I discovered through research and my practical experience as a marital and family counselor. The Bridge to Reconciliation involves four planks. We *decide* whether, how, and when to reconcile (Plank 1). Then we *discuss* the transgressions with "soft attitudes" (Plank 2). We *detoxify* our relationship of past poisons

FIGURE 7.1
The Bridge to Reconciliation

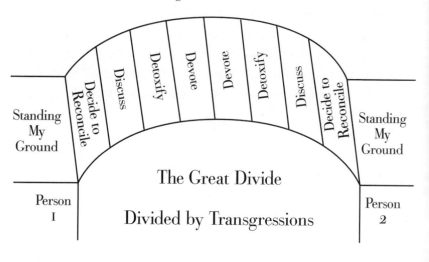

Decide to Reconcile

Discuss

Detoxify

Devote

Devote

Detoxify

Discuss

Decide to Reconcile

Standing My Ground

Standing My Ground

The Great Divide

Divided by Transgressions

Person 1

Person 2

(Plank 3). Finally, we *devote* ourselves to building up a relationship of mutual valuing (Plank 4).

Let's begin to walk across the Bridge to Reconciliation. We will examine each of the three decisions in Plank 1.

Decide *Whether* to Reconcile

WHY YOU MIGHT NOT WANT TO RECONCILE

When people have become estranged, they might not automatically want to reconcile.

- They might already have a sense of closure about the situation. "It's finished," they say. "I don't want to reopen the relationship."
- The people might like being apart.

- One person might refuse to reconcile. Reconciliation requires movement on *both* sides, so either person can block it.
- Reconciliation involves effort. One or both might not be willing to work hard enough.
- The estimated benefits of reconciling might appear to be less than the costs.

Reconciliation entails risk. People put their time, effort, and egos on the line when they try to repair trust. Granting forgiveness is risky. We risk being taken advantage of. Even thinking about reconciling is risky. It requires us to consider our own part in a relationship. What if I'm to blame? What if I confess my part? Do I diffuse the other person's responsibility? Will it let him or her off the hook? Will he or she seize on this as an admission that I am totally or mostly to blame? If I admit wrongdoing and the other person doesn't, does this lower my bargaining power? Does it make it less likely that the other person will want to reconcile? Do I set myself up to clean toilets the rest of my relationship because I am now one down to the other person? These and many more risks are inherent in seeking reconciliation. It's no wonder that most people let damaged relationships, like sleeping dogs, lie. They might get bitten.

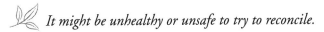 *It might be unhealthy or unsafe to try to reconcile.*

Reconciliation is not always desirable. It might be unhealthy or unsafe to try to reconcile. A woman who has been beaten repeatedly by her husband should not put herself back in harm's way until he has had help and it's safe to return. A child who has been sexually abused should be protected from the abuser. A man who is continually verbally abused by his boss might consider a new job. A student who is abused by a teacher should look for another class and/or get an authority to provide protection.

Reconciliation might also not be desirable if the perpetrator shows no remorse and no intention of changing his or her injurious behavior. Without, at minimum, remorse, it seems likely that trust will be violated repeatedly. Reconciliation isn't safe when it could put one of the members at serious risk for personal or psychological injury.

> *Reconciliation might also not be desirable if the perpetrator shows no remorse and no intention of changing his or her injurious behavior. Without, at minimum, remorse, it seems likely that trust will be violated repeatedly.*

Reconciliation is almost certainly not desirable if one partner has violated trust repeatedly. One woman told me a story of an unfaithful husband. He was unfaithful not once but six times. Each time she had listened to his confession, wiped away sincere tears, heard his well-intended promises never to stray again. Each time he fell. Now, after the sixth time, she had decided not to take him back. She wanted my assurance that this was the right choice.

She had to decide herself. Every person has a different threshold for attempting reconciliation. I probably would have tried a "tough love" approach earlier than betrayal number six, but each person must make a decision based on the circumstances.

Reconciliation might not be possible. A person may not be available. Maybe the person who inflicted the hurt or offense is dead, has moved far away, is in jail, is very ill, or cannot be contacted.

Reconciliation might not be prudent. Even though it may be safe and possible, reconciliation is often difficult and painful. Simply trying to reopen a relationship risks making yourself vulnerable. We become uncomfortable and awkward. Many people wish to avoid such discomfort. In addition, reconciliation might be hard to face because the hurt has simply been too deep. Perhaps it is still too fresh or too painful. You might not have worked through the event enough to want to open the possibility of discussing a restoring of trust, at least right now. Perhaps after some time has passed, the wounds will scab over. As for now, though, reconciliation might not be the wise thing to do.

With this litany of warnings, reasons, risks, and costs, it makes us wonder why anyone would ever want to reconcile. Let's listen to the voices that sing the countermelody.

Why You Might Want to Reconcile

People reconcile because they don't like to accept failed relationships. They might feel lonely or alone. They hope that reconciliation will fill the hole of loneliness in their hearts. They can treat reconciliation like a Band-Aid that covers a giant wound. Usually such efforts at patching up pain without pursuing the work of healing are ill-fated. On the other hand, people can allow the wound to cleanly heal itself. Empathy is the antiseptic. Forgiveness is the bandage keeping away threats of infection. Love is the heart pump of healing, bringing the lifeblood to nourish the relationship and absorb germs.

> *On the other hand, people can allow the wound to cleanly heal itself. Empathy is the antiseptic. Forgiveness is the bandage keeping away threats of infection. Love is the heart pump of healing, bringing the lifeblood to nourish the relationship and absorb germs.*

People reconcile because they value the other person and the relationship. They don't want to lose touch with a valued person or give up a once-rewarding relationship. They will work, fight, cry, and sacrifice for the merest chance of recovering a precious relationship. I have seen this often in marriages in which one spouse has had an affair. The wounded partner is often hurt and angry. Yet in spite of the pain, the person wants to hold on to the love they had (and often still have) and is willing to forgive. Sometimes the wounding partner recognizes his or her error and comes begging for forgiveness. Even if a blizzard of cold rejection threatens to freeze him or her out, he or she persists, fighting for love. Watching partners who have been driven apart by an affair has always been heart-wrenching for me. They struggle to bail a boatload of tears from a flood of emotions. Sometimes they sink. But sometimes they fight through to reconciliation and healing.

People reconcile because they have invested in the relationship, the other person, and children. While they might value the relationship and the person for their own sake, they also don't want to lose their investment. I have seen couples hang through some very conflicted times for the sake of their children. They care about the family, so they work through their differences, give up pet desires, and sacrifice for the love they invested in their children. If they emerged miserable, it might make one question the wisdom of their decision. But the investment in the children can be the capital that prevents marital bankruptcy.

People reconcile because they aren't willing to return to the status quo. They believe reconciliation will lead to a relationship stronger than the one that existed prior to the breach of trust. Bones heal stronger in the mended places, they reason.

People reconcile because they know that doing nothing spells disaster. It's not as if relationships get better on their own when hurts are not dealt with. They usually get worse. People who are hurt are prickly. They tend to be sensitive to new prickles. Sometimes they feel the prickles even when no prickles were intended. (That's the prickle pickle.) In most cases, pursuing forgiveness and reconciliation is likely to have a more positive outcome than doing nothing.

CLIMBING THE BARRIERS TO SEEKING RECONCILIATION

The barriers to deciding whether to reconcile are often our own thoughts, worries, and fears. Whether we are innocent victims, evil perpetrators, or (as is almost always true) both receiver and giver of hurts, our thought patterns can erect barriers that seem insurmountable.

We usually listen carefully to the fear-producing chatter in our heads. Now it's time to talk back! As a young boy, I always wanted to talk back to authorities, but somehow it never seemed like the smart thing to do. Now it is.

We must scale the unreasonable barriers that prevent us from seeking to restore redeemable relationships. We scale those barriers by identifying the negative and fear-producing thoughts, then arguing back at them.

In Tables 7.2 and 7.3, I identify six barriers to seeking reconciliation if you are the wounded one, and seven barriers to seeking reconciliation if you dished out more hurt than you received. In each table, I list ways you can talk back.

Check out each list. See if any of the thoughts sound familiar. If you recognize one or more, read my suggestion for talking back. Even better, make up several counterarguments yourself. See yourself as a defense attorney defending yourself from the evil prosecutor who wants to see you remain alone and estranged.

TABLE 7.2

Are Any of These Barriers Holding You Back from Seeking Reconciliation After You Have Been Hurt?

BARRIERS	HOW TO CLIMB THE BARRIERS
I don't want to give up my right to see him or her suffer.	Ask yourself, "Do I really have a *right* to see him or her suffer? Will seeing him or her in pain lessen my own pain, or might it add to my own pain?"
I don't want to give up my right to punish him or her.	Ask yourself, "Will I really feel better if I hurt him or her? Or will that lower me to his or her standards or below?"
I feel morally superior. I don't want to give that up.	Ask yourself, "Is feeling morally superior helping to restore the relationship? Could you relate better as people, both of whom make mistakes? Do you really want to continue keeping score?"
I feel vulnerable to being hurt or rejected again.	Assess the likelihood. Do not put yourself in danger. But realize that love does not happen without risk. It is taking the risk and finding the other person trustworthy that makes love special.
I'm afraid that I won't be holding him or her accountable.	Ask yourself, "Did holding him or her accountable prevent the previous transgression? Forgiveness this time does not mean that repeated transgressions have no consequences."
I'm still in too much pain. I need time to heal.	How much time do you need? We all need time to heal, but we cannot let that prevent us from ever trying to reconcile. Set a time that you think will be sufficient and revisit the decision after that time has elapsed.

TABLE 7.3
Are Any of These Barriers Holding You Back from Seeking Reconciliation If You Hurt the Other Person?

BARRIERS	HOW TO CLIMB THE BARRIERS
I don't want to admit, even to myself, that I am capable of doing such acts.	It's difficult to admit we're human. We all do things we aren't proud of, even downright ashamed of. Admitting you're capable of harming others is the first step in harming others less often.
It's embarrassing to admit to him or her that I did wrong.	Can you admit to yourself that you are embarrassed at not facing up to your acts? You'll be embarrassed either way. If you face up to your acts, though, at least you can look yourself in the mirror.
I know I was justified in my acts.	Believing you were completely justified in your acts may make you feel self-righteous, but it usually overlooks the truth that there are two sides to every story. Remember that we all make self-serving misperceptions.
I can't say, "I was wrong." It shows I'm weak.	Realize this: If you're having a hard time saying you were wrong, then saying you are wrong takes more courage and strength than if you keep it to yourself.
What if he or she refuses to forgive me?	That will be difficult. But that reflects badly on the other person, not on you. You cannot control the other person's behavior. If you sincerely sought forgiveness, you did the right thing.

continued

BARRIERS	HOW TO CLIMB THE BARRIERS
The other person might use my admission of guilt against me later.	True. The other person might use your wrong behavior against you later. Usually, a sincere apology coupled with an effort to make things right can head off many angry reprisals, but this is a risk you must judge knowing the person involved.
The other person might extract some horrid restitution because I harmed him or her.	While you will want to do whatever is reasonable to make things right, you need not accept being degraded as a person. If the other person suggests an atonement that you simply cannot do, you can make a counteroffer.

GET OVER THE FICTION THAT IF YOU GET JUSTICE, IT WILL LEAD TO RECONCILIATION

When misunderstandings, offenses, or injustices have occurred, people's natural response is to seek justice—to restore the balance that was upset. Achieving justice is no guarantee that reconciliation will occur. For example, in the book *A Time to Kill*, by John Grisham, and the movie made from it, a town was enraged by the vicious rape and attempted murder of a preadolescent African-American girl by two adult white men. The girl's father felt certain that justice would not be done because the town was primarily white. He doubted whether a jury would convict the two perpetrators. He took justice into his own hands.

As the rapists were taken to the courthouse, the father blasted them with his shotgun in front of a hundred witnesses. He was quickly apprehended without attempting to get away. A trial took place. Clearly the father killed the rapist. But was he *guilty*? Would convicting him be just or unjust? At that point, the main question is raised: Is there a time to kill? Was true justice served by the father's vigilante justice? Will the criminal justice system recognize this as a just outcome?

The movie unfolded with both sides of the conflict rallying support. In the climactic scene at the end of the movie, the two sides faced off in front of the courthouse as they awaited the verdict in the father's trial. Racial tension crackled.

"Not guilty!" said the court. The justice system had spoken clearly: There is a time to kill. Did justice lead to reconciliation? No. Violence erupted into a bloodbath.

Justice rarely leads to reconciliation, even when justice can be achieved (such as with a fair trial). At best, it brings an uneasy truce.

In most relationships, justice is never really experienced. When one side believes justice has been done, the other side doesn't. If you want to reconcile, you must *decide*. I have outlined the general reasons to reconcile or not. It's up to you to read those, look the pros and cons squarely in the eye, and decide. You can experience empathy, follow the Pyramid Model to REACH Forgiveness, and walk away. Sometimes that's the only sane thing to do. Or you can count the costs and start walking across your side of the Bridge to Reconciliation toward a meeting place somewhere near the center.

THE COSTS OF A HARD ATTITUDE

Because it's difficult either to seek forgiveness if we did wrong or to grant forgiveness if we were wronged, we usually find it easier to ignore and avoid forgiveness and reconciliation. We might try to ignore a problem or blame it on our partner. I call this a "hard attitude." We demand that we are right and that the other person should see things our way. That hard attitude has costs.

- It makes the other person want to argue back.
- It makes the other person angry.
- It focuses the other person on trying to prove that you are wrong and he or she is right.
- It has an effect opposite to what you wanted, which is to get the other person to see that you are right.
- It creates more distance between you rather than more closeness.

CLOSED FIST OR OUTSTRETCHED HAND?

As you read this in your favorite armchair, these costs of a hard attitude seem prohibitive. We can easily see that demanding the other person's sword in surrender will almost never work.

We can easily see that demanding the other person's sword in surrender will almost never work.

Yet face-to-face, it's a different story. Our wounded pride pushes self-protective buttons. When we feel vulnerable, we hunch our shoulders, ball our fists, and pull up a hard shell. When we feel insulted, we defend ourselves. Sometimes the best defense seems like a preemptive strike. Pain and threat activate our primitive drive to survive. We see the person who hurt us as the threat—the enemy.

But we have an equally basic drive—to affiliate with others to achieve a common purpose. People who are threatened seek strength in numbers. That is also a drive to survive.

So we have a choice. We can make a fist or make a friend. We can seek revenge or seek reconciliation.

So we have a choice. We can make a fist or make a friend. We can seek revenge or seek reconciliation.

It's not always best to push the affiliation button. Some threats and hurts are truly dangerous and must be defended against by distancing instead of huddling together. We need the presence of mind to let the surge of adrenaline that accompanies conflict to activate our discerning mind instead of pushing our button either to attack, avoid, or affiliate.

Decide *How* to Reconcile

Getting Back Together Without Talking About It

Most reconciliation takes place implicitly rather than explicitly. If we had to discuss every little slight, offense, or insult that occurred, productive social interaction would likely come to a halt. Talk about reconciliation would be the center of most conversation. We usually reconcile without talking about it. This is called *implicit reconciliation.* It occurs several ways.

Stop hostilities. We can realize that conflict, anger, and revenge are counterproductive, and adopt a strategy of peaceful coexistence. We can agree to disagree. By deliberate choice, we decide to get along. We bury the hatchet. Similarly, without thinking much about it, we might lose the hatchet. We could talk with the person and work with the person. Then one day we realize that the hurt and anger have decreased. We can also make a principled decision to reconcile because reconciliation is consonant with our social philosophy, religious beliefs, and values. Maybe we decide to reconcile because we simply believe that reconciliation is the right thing to do and remaining estranged is the wrong thing to do.

Come together. We can also work together on a common task. Meeting challenges and working toward common goals help people rebuild trust. In a closely related way, we can reconcile through doing pleasing activities together. Parents and children often put aside relationship strains after playing, hiking, watching television, or reading together. Spouses sometimes find that making love washes away relationship tension.

Two together equals one plus one plus one. Sometimes a third person can help. When siblings conflict, the parent might play with one sibling, invite the second sibling to join, and then exit the situation leaving the two siblings playing together. Adults do the equivalent at cocktail parties by joining up two other adults, engaging them in conversation, then moving on.

Be positive. We can reconcile through complimenting, stroking, or making each other feel good psychologically.

Forgive and reconcile. We can reconcile and thus trust each other again because we have healed our wounds through forgiving.

The trouble with implicit reconciliation is that it can be easily misunderstood. When we *say* we want to reconcile, the other person might disagree or not want to accept our approach. But at least he or she knows our intent. When you decide to try implicit reconciliation, the other person might not know that you're trying to reconcile. If you offer to work on a task together, you might be hoping that you can repair the relationship. The other person might believe you are trying to bribe or "guilt" him or her, so reconciliation fizzles. You might initiate sex in the hope of reconciling. Your partner might say afterward, "Thank you very much for the sex. I feel less horny, but I'm outta here." Remember, implicit reconciliation often works. It is kinder and gentler than explicit reconciliation. But it is more easily misinterpreted.

Sometimes it's better to be explicit. The Bridge to Reconciliation—you're midway across Plank 1 as you make these decisions—is one method of explicit reconciliation. See Table 7.4 for guidelines about deciding the right time to reconcile.

Decide *When* to Reconcile

If you decide to reconcile and you know how you wish to do it, the question of timing still remains. Remember the simple truth: Reconciliation is a process, not an event, because reconciliation requires rebuilding of mutual trust, which takes time. Forgiveness can sometimes be granted instantly. Reconciliation almost always requires a time during which people are wary of each other. They walk softly (and often carry a big stick). They hope for a hug but prepare for a punch.

> *Reconciliation almost always requires a time during which people are wary of each other. They walk softly (and often carry a big stick). They hope for a hug but prepare for a punch.*

Look for a good time to make a tentative first step toward reconciling. Don't wait for the other person to take the initiative. People who have hurt each other often have wounded pride, which makes them hesitate. You can starve to death emotionally while waiting for an estranged person to feed you. So you will usually want to make the first move.

Be careful, especially if the other person's pride was wounded. One way that people restore a diminished sense of self-esteem is to attack and defeat another person—and you can step onto their radar screen. Just as dangerous, examine your own heart. Have you been hurt? Do you harbor an urge to vindicate yourself? Your desire to "discuss the issue"—ostensibly to reconcile—might be camouflage for attack.

When are you most likely to want to reconcile? Perhaps it's when you feel guilty over some misdeed. Perhaps it's when you

TABLE 7.4

Guidelines for Deciding When to Try Implicit
Reconciliation and When to Continue Across the
Bridge to Reconciliation

What You Think or Feel	What to Do
I am really, *really* torqued off.	Let your adrenaline be a cue for you to think, not act. You may eventually talk about the issue, but first cool off.
The situation doesn't lend itself to long talks (e.g., at work).	Try avoiding the person until some time passes, burying the hatchet, opting for peaceful coexistence, or working on a task together.
The person holds power over me.	Is the person vindictive? Be careful. Proceed across the Bridge with caution. Perhaps you need to try to regain some trust through working peacefully together before you talk.
I am in a position of authority over the other person.	Again, walk cautiously. Attempts to force a conversation can be perceived as coercion—regardless of how gentle you are.
We have a history of conflict.	Try implicit reconciliation. If that doesn't work, move to the Bridge. Emphasize your own vulnerability rather than attacking.
We have a history of being able to forgive and to reconcile.	Proceed across the Bridge to Reconciliation.
We don't seem to be able to read each other's intentions accurately.	Proceed across the Bridge to Reconciliation.

What You Think or Feel	What to Do
I am very hurt.	Soft emotions, such as vulnerability and hurt, usually inhibit the other person from strongly attacking. When you feel hurt (but are not seething with anger), you often will be more likely to reconcile through crossing the Bridge than through sulking.
I am stressed to the limit.	Don't even think about bringing up a transgression.
I'm frustrated. I haven't had my say.	You probably don't really want to discuss; you want to talk. If you move to Plank 2, discipline yourself before you launch into your own story. If you charge ahead with a monologue, you'll vent but probably drive the other person away.

think of how badly you feel when disappointment separates you from your partner, friend, or coworker. Perhaps it's when you see others enjoying close relationships.

Two warning signs signal you to wait before trying to reconcile. When you're extremely stressed, it often doesn't take much of a bump on the track to derail your good intentions. When you're seething and feel you haven't been able to get your say, you are probably poised for a fight. In either case, take a few deep breaths and let things calm down before you move to reconcile.

If you feel like you're on an emotional roller coaster, expect the other person to feel the same way. Use your skills at empathy. Ask yourself whether the other person is stressed or furious. Does he or she feel the pull to talk softly or to pull you by the neck? If the conditions are right, go for it.

TAKING THE PLUNGE

Taking the plunge into explicit reconciliation requires that you talk about the transgression. This is like entering a minefield, especially if both partners are sensitized to the negative. How do you talk about the transgression, forgiveness, and reconciliation productively? How do you discuss getting back together in relative safety without an explosion of conflict?

> *Taking the plunge into explicit reconciliation requires that you talk about the transgression. This is like entering a minefield, especially if both partners are sensitized to the negative.*

In many ongoing relationships, reconciliation can occur because people forgive. In others, people forgive because they have already reconciled. There is not one single way to reconcile effectively. The Bridge to Reconciliation can help, but it's both difficult and risky. And the hardest and riskiest part is Plank 2, discussion. This is where the bridge is most likely to crumble. Or it can stretch farther across the trust gap.

Do you have one or more trust gaps in your life? Have you decided to attempt to reconcile? Have you decided to address the issues explicitly? If so, before you decide that now is the time, make sure you understand the next plank: discussion.

CHAPTER 8

Discussion

The public form of forgiveness is reconciliation. And
this is of necessity a much longer, more complex process. . . .
Reconciliation entails several stages: repentance, contrition,
acceptance of responsibility, healing, and finally reunion.
—JOHN T. PAWLIKOWSKI

Once upon a time, two people lived together in blissful harmony. They never said a cross word to each other and were always supportive and loving. They valued each other completely. One day, one partner simply hauled off and betrayed the other person.

You undoubtedly recognized right away that the above story is my hallucination (no doubt brought on by too much chunky peanut butter). In reality, we all know that when two people live together, perfection cannot exist. People at times accidentally or purposely hurt each other. Over time, a history of wounds accumulates in people's backgrounds, regardless of how good their relationship is. The number and severity of wounds might be insignificant compared with the loving acts in the couple's lives, but there is always a background of wounds that have been treated with forbearance, ignored, accepted, forgiven, and often forgotten.

Furthermore, whenever people do hurt each other, they don't often inflict the hurt out of the blue, with evil intentions. They might not even be aware they caused pain. They might have felt provoked by the other person, stressed, frustrated, cranky from lack of sleep, maybe even constipated. Transgressions always have two sides.

Of course, transgressions have two sides—except when I'm in the heat of battle. Then forget it. I'm right! If I acknowledge the other person's point, I feel downright unpatriotic. There is a sense of disloyalty to myself in admitting that I might have been partly to blame for a hurt that I received. To protect myself, I harden my attitude. I am right. Period.

> *Of course, transgressions have two sides—except when I'm in the heat of battle. Then forget it. I'm right!*

Unfortunately, a hard attitude spells disaster for reconciliation. To reconcile, I must create a soft attitude and engage in soft talk about the hurt. Having a soft attitude requires that you admit to yourself that there are two sides to *this* conflict and to *this* hurt. Admitting to yourself the two sides of the conflict is the mere beginning. You then must convey this to your partner.

Soften Your Attitude

Many people blame the other person for whatever goes wrong. This is a fact of human nature. People tend not to focus on their own character. For example, if you see Joey hit a person, chase him, scream loudly, and throw cold water on him, you will probably say that Joey is aggressive and cruel. But if Joey explains his own behavior, he won't say that he is aggressive and cruel. He'll say, "That guy insulted my wife and children, and I gave him what he deserved." It is natural for people involved in a conflict to explain their actions by referring to what the other person did, because the other person's behavior is easier for them to see.

We almost always see the other person as the perpetrator. Greg Jones, dean of the divinity school at Duke University, says, "In many situations, the possibility of reconciliation has been eliminated because both parties (or all the parties) come prepared to forgive and are completely unprepared to be forgiven."[1] Sometimes we can admit we have done wrong, but usually we all feel like victims.

Therefore two self-identified victims are usually found in relationships, both blaming the other. Both "victims" usually believe that they perceive the events correctly. The other person is, thus, wrong (at best) or lying (at worst).

Unfortunately, both are usually equally wrong in their perceptions, as shown in an experiment by psychologists A. M. Stillwell and Roy F. Baumeister in 1997.[2] In that study, three groups of people were read the same long story about an offense that took place between a victim and a perpetrator. The situation, offense, reactions, and the consequences for both parties were described. One group was told simply to remember what they heard. The second group was told to listen as if they were the perpetrator. The third group was told to listen as if they were the victim. The researchers later tallied and compared the number of errors in factual memory among the three groups. The fewest errors were made by the people who listened objectively. Surprisingly, the people who listened as victim or perpetrator made the same number of errors in memory. However, they made dramatically different kinds of errors. "Perpetrators" remembered the victim's provocations. They remembered their own decisions to stop attacking the victim. They minimized the consequences to the victim. When the victim said that the event didn't really bother him or her, the perpetrator took that at face value. On the other hand, while "victims" made as many mistakes as perpetrators, they overlooked their own provocations of the perpetrator. They remembered asking the perpetrator to stop the attacks. They remembered their own pain. So both victim and perpetrator unintentionally distorted their memories in self-serving ways. This tendency of human nature hardens people's attitudes against reconciliation. By understanding this, perhaps we can be more humble. What we perceive and believe to be correct might not be totally accurate.

> *So both victim and perpetrator unintentionally distorted their memories in self-serving ways. This tendency of human nature hardens people's attitudes against reconciliation.*

Soft Attitudes That Help You Talk Softly

EMPATHY

We already know that empathy for the one who hurt us will help us forgive the person. If we are to let go of our hatred and replace negative emotions with positive ones, we need to feel what the other person might have felt.

> *Empathy is just as crucial for seeking forgiveness as for giving it.*

Empathy is also important if we have hurt or offended someone. We need to put ourselves in the shoes of the victim in order
to ask him or her to forgive us. Empathy is just as crucial for seeking forgiveness as for giving it.

Steve Sandage headed a team in our lab that studied college
students and sought to predict who would and would not seek
forgiveness when they had wronged someone.[3] The strongest pre-
dictor of unwillingness to seek forgiveness was inability or unwillingness to empathize with others. Unforgiving people often failed
to see how much they hurt others. They could not imagine others' suffering, so they could not imagine that they might need to
apologize.

Empathy can help us forgive and seek forgiveness, and it plays
another crucial role in reconciliation. If we see that the other person is empathic toward us, we feel understood. That makes us
want to patch up a tattered relationship. Let me illustrate the
power of feeling understood.

At a conference for counselors in 1996, I spoke on forgiveness.
I talked about the death of my mom and how I forgave by empathizing with the murderer. After my talk, several in the audi-
ence began to share with me their stories of giving and getting
forgiveness. Out of the corner of my eye, I noticed a woman who
held herself apart while others stepped forward to talk. At one
point I looked at the woman, but she gave a little head shake.
Someone else filled the gap. Finally, everyone in the room had
spoken except for that woman.

"I feel new hope," she told us. "When I heard you describe
what you thought the boy who murdered your mom might have
felt, I cried. My son . . ." She stopped, choked up. A tear tumbled
down her cheek. She tried again. "My son broke into a woman's

house and killed her. He was convicted of murder. Having just turned eighteen, he must serve his sentence in adult prison."

Again she struggled to go on. "Added to my heartsickness, people in our community could not accept my husband and me. They would see us at church but not speak. They would see us in the grocery store and head down a different aisle. We felt isolated. No friends. Even people at the PTA seemed to shun us." She seemed to be trying for a little humor, but it fell flat.

"Frankly, my husband and I had about given up. We've seriously considered moving to another state where no one has heard of us. No one could understand. No one. People say the most hateful things. They say, 'How could you raise such a monster?' They treat us as if we taught our son to murder."

I made an encouraging murmur. "It feels like nobody cares," I said.

"They don't. They can't understand. He grew up as a good boy. He did the usual adolescent pranks. He wasn't perfect. He was normal. I've been a counselor for almost twenty years. I've seen hundreds of adolescents. He was *normal.*"

She paused. It was almost as if she stood at the edge of a diving board, uncertain about whether to leap. "Then the night that ruined his life came. He broke into a house for thrills. But while he and his friends were robbing the house, the woman who lived there came home. He attacked her and she died.

"Until you talked today, I didn't think that anyone could ever understand what might have been going on in his life when he committed that murder. Hearing you describe your experience with such empathy and compassion changed me. Your understanding of the boy who murdered your mother gave me hope. I now believe that *someone* can understand. If one person can, then others can.

"My husband and I have cut ourselves off from the community since people have given us the cold shoulder. I see that I need to try to forgive those people who have reacted to the horror of the murder. They don't understand what they are doing to my husband and me. Jesus said, 'Forgive them, for they know not what they do.' I've known all along that I should forgive, but . . ." She struggled for the words to express her feelings. "But when I heard that you could understand and even forgive, it gave me the courage to try to make things right with people who used to be friends."

One of the difficult parts of being a speaker is that we meet interesting and courageous people such as this woman. We walk with them for a short way, but we don't get to see the rest of their story. I, of course, wished her and her family well. My hope is that her story can help others to persevere and to reconcile.

So many people carry enormous pain. We have no idea of the load others might be wrestling with. When we choose to empathize, sometimes that can be the key to lift their burden enough so they can take steps toward seeing and admitting their own unforgiveness. It might even lead to reconciliation.

You Can If They Can

Remember Rosalie Gerut from Chapter 3? She is the wonderful, charismatic Jewish woman whose mother survived the Holocaust. Rosalie cofounded the organization One by One. Her organization helps children of Holocaust survivors and children of Nazi SS soldiers to begin conversations that eventually lead to healing. Her method is based on getting people together in a room. Formerly faceless "enemies" then have human faces. They can share their stories with each other. By listening to the stories of the struggles that people from "the other side" have to tell, a deep sense of empathy can build within the group, and people can become open to being reconciled with others whom they had previously thought badly of. The One by One philosophy can promote reconciliation and healing. It is based on openness, honesty, and empathy. If children of Nazis and Jewish Holocaust survivors can talk and empathize, you can too.

HERE'S AN IMAGE TO SHAKE YOUR PRIDE

Pride is a hard attitude that often trips reconciliation at the starting gate. Whenever I begin to feel prideful, I use a vivid story to deflate my swelled head. Unfortunately, I have forgotten the source of the story.

A young man was in his college dormitory room lifting weights. He glanced in the mirror and saw that his muscles were bulging from having pumped iron. Feeling like Arnold Schwarzenegger, he decided to head to the student union and "give the women a treat." (Did I mention that humility was not his strong suit?) He slipped his sleeveless tank top over his naked torso and headed out the door. At the last moment, as he glanced in the mirror, he thought, *The scholar-athlete will be much more impressive than the mere athlete.* He hefted a few textbooks and tucked the six weightiest under his arm. (He had finally found a use for Gray's *Anatomy.*) Glancing in the mirror, he noticed that the scholar-athlete look had the side benefit of causing his biceps to bulge.

He swaggered into the student union, where he bought an all-American college meal: burger, fries, and shake. Balancing the tray with one hand and his six books with the other, he headed toward an open seat across the cafeteria. He knew instinctively that every woman in the room probably was looking at him. *I'm cool,* he thought.

He noticed several young women whom he wanted to impress, so he casually leaned down to drink from his straw . . . and missed. Embarrassed, he lunged at the straw again. It bounced off his lip. His straining lips and thrusting tongue chased that pesky straw around and around in circles. Frustrated and embarrassed, he opened his mouth and lurched at the straw. It bounced off his lip and lodged in his right nostril. Not cool. He wiggled his nose, to no avail. He shook his head. He sniffed (bad idea). He blew. No luck. In desperation, he jerked his head backward, but the straw came with him. He became the Amazing Man with the Straw in His Nose—a legend in his own time. Swinging his head from side to side, he did a sort of Jackson Pollock–like milkshake splatter painting of all the people sitting nearby. He was a popular guy.

"Pride goeth before a fall," said the writer of Proverbs. Remembering the Amazing Man with the Straw in His Nose has helped me keep my pride under control many times.

Pride is a significant barrier to asking for forgiveness and seeking reconciliation. Even when people know they're in the wrong, it's hard to admit it to someone else.

Pride is a significant barrier to asking for forgiveness and seeking reconciliation.

HUMILITY

Developing humility is more than merely defeating pride. At least one psychologist, June Price Tangney, has begun to think scientifically about researching humility.[4] Initial efforts have not been promising. Humility is enormously difficult for psychologists to investigate. Imagine the dilemma. Suppose I ask people on a questionnaire, "Are you humble?" If they answer yes, it's almost proof that they aren't humble. If they answer no, they might be truly humble. Then again, they might simply have self-esteem lower than a worm's belly button. So humility is difficult to investigate and even to conceptualize.

True humility is not defeating pride. It is thinking of the other person. Researchers believe that the characteristics of empathy and humility and the absence of pride are the character traits that most predict a person's being willing to risk seeking forgiveness.

> *True humility is not defeating pride. It is thinking of the other person.*

You can cultivate humility by understanding that you might not be as correct as you think you are. It's a simple matter of perception.

How to Keep Your Cool

PRACTICE EMPATHY WHILE THE OTHER PERSON EXPLAINS

When the other person explains his or her point of view, try to see things from that point of view. That is, practice empathizing. The natural reaction when you disagree is to argue mentally as the other person tries to explain. That is the road to a heated exchange. Instead, stay cool. Try to understand the pressures, stresses, and special circumstances that influenced the person to hurt you. Keep the focus off yourself.

SUMMARIZE WHAT THE OTHER PERSON SAYS

Practice your empathic listening skills, reflecting what the other person said and what his or her feelings were. Let the person know that you accurately understand what he or she was feeling and thinking. This is called active listening.

For instance, Sharon says, "I can't stand being here when you criticize me. It drives me absolutely nuts. I feel violent inside. I want to run away screaming. That's why I left and slammed the door. I was afraid of what I'd do if I stuck around."

Margo replies, "You hear me say something critical and it hurts you. You feel angry—so angry you have to get away fast. Just a few minutes ago that anger made you leave and slam the door. Am I understanding you?"

GIVE THE PERSON THE BENEFIT OF THE DOUBT

Few people try to hurt someone they care about. In fact, almost no one tries to hurt or offend strangers or even rivals. Most hurts are due to misunderstandings, unusual stresses, or striking back in quick anger from a presumed provocation. Instead of assuming that the person who hurt you is malevolent, evil, and the chief emissary of the Dark Side of the Force, give the person the benefit of the doubt and assume he or she had positive motives. Misunderstandings usually happen not because people's motives are evil, but because they aren't effective in turning their positive motives into positive actions.

For instance, Kirby recently had one of those terrible, horrible, no-good, very bad days. She was in the backyard shed where we keep our clothes dryer. As she checked to see whether the clothes were dry, she continued to tell me about her horrible day. She paused to open the dryer. I stepped into the backyard to pick up a limb that had fallen from the tree.

"Where did you go?" she said, clearly hurt. "I was still talking."

I apologized. "I thought you had finished for now. You said we would talk more as we walked around the neighborhood."

"I didn't ever stop talking."

"You turned your back. I guess I didn't hear. Sorry."

As we talked further during our walk, I said, "You know I love you, so you know I didn't get up this morning and say, 'I think I'll reject the person I love.' "

"Yes, I do know that. But I didn't feel that," she said. "I felt rejected. Because I know you love me, and because I feel that now we're talking about it, I can give you the benefit of the doubt. My head knew you loved me, but my heart didn't know what to do with the feelings."

BE FAIR IN YOUR EXPECTATIONS

You want to be fair, but nature is working against you. You naturally see things from your own point of view, not from the other person's point of view. Therefore, you see the costs that you've incurred more clearly than the costs to the other person.

It takes work to cultivate empathy for the other person. It requires effort to be humble. But it's well worth it. Act with the knowledge that he or she is the same under the skin as you are. You might naturally expect the person who hurt you to grovel contritely. Not a humble expectation. Or you might naturally expect that the other person will offer to pay you one million dollars in restitution—not likely to occur. But if you examine things from the other person's point of view, you will be able to create a more realistic expectation that will keep you from being disappointed.

CONSIDER FORGIVING

If the other person has admitted wrongdoing, apologized, and offered restitution, then the burden has been placed upon you to consider granting forgiveness. Some people think that the transgressor should be thoroughly repentant before they are obligated to forgive. That is, they believe forgiveness should be granted only after a person has given evidence that he or she is going to change direction and act positively. Others, including myself, advocate forgiveness without requiring repentance. For me, the issue is one of humility. I have found it hard to know my own motives. I know how weak I am. I sincerely *want* to act positively toward someone who might have offended me, or whom I have often offended. But a negative thought creeps in, or a critical word, and I "forget" to be nice. All the time, I sincerely want to rise above any tension between us and take the high road.

So when I start feeling like I want to see true repentance before I'm willing to forgive, I come up against my own weaknesses, foibles, and failures. If I cannot expect unfailing repentance from myself, how can I expect it from someone else? Even worse, if I can't even know my own motives, then how can I presume to judge the other person's true motives? How can I say to myself, "He isn't *really* sorry for what he did," or "He's just pretending"?

Out of the humility of knowing my own limitations, then, I want to err on the side of forgiving too easily. I want to be quick to forgive.

Decide If You Should Give or Get Forgiveness—or Both

Who's responsible for seeking reconciliation if a hurt or misunderstanding has occurred? If we value the relationship, both people should want to do whatever they can to restore their closeness. Even if the other person doesn't seem to want to act, don't wait for him or her to initiate reconciliation. Relationships are too precious to give up on them easily. Clearly, you don't want to become a doormat by not holding the other person accountable for his or her behavior. On the other hand, giving tit for tat will rarely restore a relationship. You must find your balance—not an easy thing to do.

Keeping your cool in a two-sided disagreement is very hard to do. It challenges you to employ the virtues you want to build in yourself—even in the face of provocation. Empathize. Look first to understand rather than be understood. Give the other person the benefit of the doubt. Be fair and be humble. If you can do most of those things most of the time when you feel provoked, you can keep your cool.

Examine Your *Acts*

Before you launch into a discussion with someone who wounded you, identify clearly what you believe he or she did that wronged you. That sounds obvious, but when we are wronged, we *feel* but don't always *think*. I usually want to react rather than plan a response. When I do react, though, I'm usually sorry later.

So be sure you can say exactly what was wrong *before* you say it. Practice when you're alone. How does it sound when you say it aloud? Remember, you can say the same thing with vinegar or honey. As long as you're alone, it might also be helpful to think about why the other person might have acted as he or she did. Start the motor of empathy.

Resolve to examine your own part in the hurt before you discuss it. Think about what, if anything, you might have done to provoke the other person. What was the person seeing and hearing? What was the background with which he or she entered the situation? Was the person frazzled because of stress at work, driven to distraction by demands from children or friends, or attempting to cope with a list of fifty activities to complete before lunchtime?

Then examine how you responded to the person's actions. What did you say when he or she hurt you? What did you feel? What did you do? Did you get defensive and lash back with harsh words? Think about how your acts might have made the person feel and how you might have felt if you had been him or her.

Finally, examine what you've done since the incident. Have you retaliated? Sulked? Slammed doors? Ignored the person? Failed to look him or her in the eye—or stared hard in hatred? Have you been accommodating? Perhaps you simply smiled and let the incident pass, seemingly unperturbed, so that the person has no clue you're still upset about the hurt. To the other person, your actions might feel mean and hateful. He or she might not connect your behavior with having caused you pain.

This self-examination shouldn't be legalistic. It shouldn't be a find-one-thing-that-I-did-wrong-so-I can-blame-my-partner type of self-examination. Rather, true self-examination tries to create an atmosphere of give-and-take and sees oneself honestly.

Make a Gentle Reproach

Now you are ready to talk about the transgression (Figure 8.1). The talk has three parts: a *reproach* by the person who feels wronged, an *account* by the wrongdoer, and a *consideration of forgiveness*. Here are some suggestions for how to do each part.

When a transgression occurs, the wronged party will usually ask for an explanation, called a *reproach*. One can make a harsh reproach, saying, "You barbarian. You have the sensitivity of gravel. How could you do such a horrid thing to me? Don't you love me?"

Now, color me cynical, but I predict that this approach will not make the relationship flourish. It's just a hunch, mind you.

FIGURE 8.1
Soft Talk About Transgressions

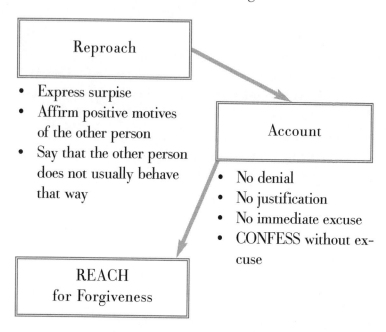

On the other hand, a gentle reproach might say, "When you insulted me, I was surprised. You're usually very sensitive. Can you tell me what was going on?" A gentle reproach affirms the person's positive motives and usual positive behavior. It asks for an explanation from the other person's point of view. It is respectful, and it will usually keep the door open for genuine dialogue.

Give a Soft Answer

How you reproach the other person will affect the type of explanation you get. Some answers are "hard." Others are "soft."

Let's put the shoe on the other foot for a moment. Suppose you have erred. Perhaps you're ashamed. You think desperately for an excuse. You know the reproach is soon to come. You will soon have to give an account for your behavior. What are your options? There are four types of answers: denials, justifications, excuses, and concessions.

DENIALS

You can *deny* that anything was wrong. The person says, "You hurt me." You say, "I didn't hurt you." Or you say, "You shouldn't have been hurt by *that*." That's a denial.

JUSTIFICATIONS

Or you could *justify* what was done. A justification is admitting that you did wrong but saying that it was okay and morally right to do the act. By justifying yourself, you imply, "Anyone would have done as I did." For example, you might say, "Sure, I insulted you, but it was because you insulted me first." That's a justification. It says, "I had a legal and/or moral right to do what I did." When we justify ourselves, it's almost always because we think we are simply responding as any sane person would have responded. We make move number one in the blame game.

EXCUSES

The third possibility is to *excuse* yourself for the act. This type of answer says, "I did wrong, but there were compelling reasons for doing wrong." For instance, you might excuse yourself by saying, "Sure, I insulted you, but it was because I was under huge stress. My boss gave me ten jobs to do today. The children were each disciplined at school and sent home. Our dog bit a lawyer's child.

The IRS has notified me that I am going to be audited tomorrow, and I had spinach on my front tooth when I talked to the president of the company this afternoon. Therefore, I cannot be held accountable for a little insult." Excuses say, "I was wrong. I should have known better. However, these compelling reasons might at least make my actions understandable."

Confessions

The fourth type of account is called a *confession*. You confess to wrongdoing and concede that you have done wrong. You do not attempt to justify or excuse the behavior.

Which one is most effective?

If we've done wrong, we'll feel best if we deny our wrongdoing—assuming we really don't feel that we did anything wrong. If we're trying to cover up, that's a different story. Denial works best for our feelings if we really believe we are innocent. However, denial is tough on our relationships.

If we deny wrongdoing, the other person will usually be livid. By denying—no matter how tactfully we did it—we spit in the person's eye. We say, "I can't believe you're accusing me! You were wrong. You were even stupid for accusing me. Take it back." The other person's options are few: fight or flight. Neither is going to help the relationship be stronger.

What should we do if we truly believe the reproach was incorrect? Assume that the person is feeling hurt or angry for a good reason. Find out why. Instead of denying, say, "You seem pretty angry. What happened? I want to know."

Then we must listen carefully—not to pick holes in the argument, but to understand the person's experience.

If we justify ourselves by blaming the other person, we will feel less wrong, but the blame game is a no-win situation. It catapults us into an argument 99 percent of the time. Unless we thrive on conflict, we will probably pay a large price for blaming the other person.

> *If we justify ourselves by blaming the other person, we will feel less wrong, but the blame game is a no-win situation.*

When we say, "I did wrong but I was justified because you did wrong first," we take a weak moral stance. We are in effect saying, "Two wrongs make a right." Logically, we would never agree to such a position. But arguments seem to use logic only as a blunt instrument to pound the other person with. Emotion seems to be the driving force. By taking the two-wrongs-make-a-right stance, we open ourselves to be pounded.

Instead of jumping in with a justification or blaming the other person, we should listen. Hear the other person out. If we believe the other person provoked us, we would be wise to deal with our own misbehavior *before* we try to correct the other person.

If we truly believe that we have some good excuses for our behavior, we would be wise to share those with the other person. Yet how we frame it is crucial. When we say, "Sure, I insulted you, but . . . ," it really doesn't matter what we say next. When the person hears us say *but,* he or she turns off. I recall being in a group with an elderly woman who had a hearing aid. Whenever someone said something she didn't agree with, she dramatically reached up, turned off her hearing aid, leaned back, and smiled. The word *but* is an off switch to a hearing aid.

Telling the other person about the pressures we were

experiencing will promote empathy and help the person REACH forgiveness. Remember, that's precisely what the person needs to do to forgive us—empathize with all the pressures that we were under. Yet the *but* that precedes a litany of excuses is a hot button that clicks off the emotional hearing aid and sends that person into attack mode. When we say, "I insulted you, but . . . ," it says to the person, "I insulted you, but I have no clue how much it hurt you or how angry it made you. All I care about is that you understand *me* and the pressure *I* was under." So if we make immediate excuses, it suggests that we are insensitive and self-focused. It triggers (1) blame, (2) more explanations about how hurt or offended the person was, and (3) a hard attitude not receptive to reconciling.

> *Yet the* but *that precedes a litany of excuses is a hot button that clicks off the emotional hearing aid and sends that person into attack mode.*

So instead of making excuses, we'll have more success if we make the good confession. After we have admitted our wrongdoing fully (using the following CONFESS approach), we will be able to help the other person understand us better.

CONFESS

George forgot to put money in the checking account. Gwyn wrote a check that bounced. Because George was out of town, Gwyn had to spend an entire morning straightening out their accounts. When she mentioned it, he blew up and left the house, slamming the door. Now he's sorry. Here are seven steps to a good confession. Each begins with a letter of the acrostic CONFESS.

C = Confess Without Excuse

George needs to say, "Honey, I forgot to deposit the money in the checking account." He should make a simple confession. No excuses. No buts. If George is feeling particularly loquacious, he can even add, "I feel terrible. I'm so brain-dead sometimes."

Let's face it. It's hard to admit that we were wrong. We lose face. We can say, "I made a mistake. I miscalculated. I messed up." But somehow it's hard to come right out and say, "I was wrong." George needs to say it. "Honey, I forgot to deposit money in the checking account. I was wrong. I don't have an excuse at all. I blew it."

O = Offer an Apology

It is essential that we are sorry for what we did. An apology is one of the best ways to start reconciliation. To be effective, an apology must be specific. A general apology like "I'm sorry I hurt you" isn't very effective. A very general apology like "I'm sorry for all the times in the past that I hurt you" is even less effective.

Effective apologies are specific. George needs to say, "I'm also sorry I called you names and stormed out when you were trying to explain yourself. Deep down I knew that would hurt you, and I am really sorry that I hurt you. That was wrong too."

 *Effective apologies are specific.*

In our research, we have found that there's nothing magical about the exact words "I am sorry." Rather, to be effective, an apology must convince the other person that we feel *sincere regret* and *remorse* for doing what we did. If we can get this across, we will promote forgiveness and further reconciliation.

Why does an apology help the other person forgive us? It not only disarms the person, it also stimulates the other person to empathize with us. If we apologize and convince the other person that we are truly remorseful for what we did, it helps the person get into our shoes instead of fighting with us. They can see our pain, so they can be quicker to forgive.

N = Note His or Her Pain

"I see by your tears that I have really hurt you badly. When I wound you deeply, you seem to draw inside a protective shell. I know you were counting on my depositing the money in the checking account," says George. "You must be very disappointed with me. I also know that I wasted your time, which made you stressed and angry."

George has to let Gwyn know that he understands what she's feeling. By empathizing with Gwyn, George shows he is connected to her. His empathy lets her know he cares, which makes it easier for her to forgive him.

F = Forever Value

Love is valuing the other person. George can show he loves Gwyn by saying, "I know I didn't respect your time. I want to always value you. I'm sorry I acted so irresponsibly." George does love Gwyn. He isn't using a "technique," trying to manipulate her, or attempting to weasel out of trouble. By expressing his love and affirming that he will always feel that way, he lets her know he cares about her.

E = Equalize

Equalizing is making up for the loss that the other person experienced. To offer *restitution* is to equalize the balance of justice. Any hurt or offense causes the person who is hurt to lose something, whether it's self-esteem, self-respect, or a tangible benefit (such as if I were to offend you in front of your boss and you lose a promotion opportunity). So it is an act of kindness for the transgressor to offer to make up for the loss. George can offer to equalize. He should say, "Is there anything I can do to make up for what I have done?"

To offer restitution *is to equalize the balance of justice.*

When the transgressor spontaneously offers restitution, the victim often softens. If the victim proposes the restitution, it is usually more demanding. For example, when George offers to make restitution, if Gwyn is empathic, she will realize that making such an offer costs George something in terms of his self-esteem. Therefore, Gwyn might say that no restitution is needed, or suggest a small restitution. However, if George does *not* spontaneously offer restitution, Gwyn might say, "I think you should do something to make up for what you did. Why don't you clean the toilet for the next twenty years?" Gwyn will likely name a restitution that involves more-punitive damages because she doesn't perceive George as having incurred any cost by offering to make things right. She doesn't see that he is taking a risk that Gwyn will hammer him. In fact, by not offering to make restitution, George makes Gwyn ask for restitution, which increases the amount that she perceives herself as having lost. The bottom line: If we offend, we should offer to do something to make up for the transgression.

S = Say "Never Again"

It will help relational healing if we say that we will try not to hurt the other person in the same way again. We cannot logically promise never to hurt him or her again. Accidents happen. Events may conspire so that we do hurt people, regardless of how hard we try not to. Our positive intention—and hearing us say it aloud—is important to building trust. "I am going to do my best," says George, "to always deposit my check on the way home from work. I also don't ever want to get so angry with you and with myself that I storm out without resolving things."

S = SEEK FORGIVENESS

George must now ask for forgiveness. He should be specific. He should say, "Can you forgive me for insulting you? I'm so sorry." By asking for forgiveness, he admits clearly that he's done something that deserves condemnation. Many people walk through CONFES and cannot take the last step to the final S. "Can you f—, f—, f—, for—? You know? Can you?" George needs to look Gwyn right in the eye and say, "Honey, I don't deserve it, but can you forgive me for not respecting your time and then—to make it worse—storming out?"

In the case of mutual offenses, ask forgiveness for your own part regardless of what the other person did to hurt you. If he or she hurt you, that doesn't justify your hurting him or her. So take responsibility for your own actions. If you hurt the person, ask clearly for forgiveness. In so doing, you also acknowledge that you did wrong and that the other person has the power to forgive you for what you did.

> *If you hurt the person, ask clearly for forgiveness. In so doing, you also acknowledge that you did wrong and that the other person has the power to forgive you for what you did.*

In all of these steps thus far, you are practicing empathy. You are seeing things through the eyes of your partner. You are trying to do things that your partner would appreciate. You are demonstrating understanding of, emotional identification with, and compassion for your partner, all of which combine to make up sincere empathy.

The two hardest parts of CONFESS are usually C (confess without excuse) and the last S (seek forgiveness). Both challenge our ego.

> *The two hardest parts of CONFESS are usually C (confess without excuse) and the last S (seek forgiveness). Both challenge our ego.*

MAKING THE GOOD CONFESSION

Let's put George's confession together and hear how it sounds.

"Honey, I forgot to deposit the money in the checking account. I feel terrible. I'm so brain-dead sometimes. I was wrong. I don't have an excuse at all. I blew it. I'm also sorry I called you names and stormed out when you were trying to explain yourself. Deep down I knew that would hurt you, and I'm really sorry that I hurt you. That was wrong too.

"I see by your tears that I have really hurt you badly. When I wound you deeply, you seem to draw inside a protective shell. I know you were counting on my depositing the money in the checking account. You must be very disappointed with me. I also know that I wasted your time, which made you stressed and angry. I know I didn't respect your time. I always want to value you. I'm sorry I acted so irresponsibly.

"Is there anything I can do to make up for what I've done?"

"I am going to do my best to always deposit my check on the way home from work. I also don't ever want to get so angry with you and with myself that I storm out without resolving things. Honey, I don't deserve it, but can you forgive me for not respecting your time and then—to make it worse—storming out? Would it help you to forgive me to know what was going on with me?"

Now, Give Reasons

ASK WHETHER YOUR PARTNER WOULD LIKE TO UNDERSTAND YOUR THINKING

After—and only after—we have completely confessed our part of the interaction, we might offer the opportunity for the other person to understand the reasons why we acted as we did. We need to be careful not to justify or excuse what we did. Instead, we provide the reasons that will make our act understandable. We don't want to convey to the other person that we're making light of or worming out of our part. We are not trying to excuse our behavior.

Explaining our reasoning can help the other person empathize with us (and perhaps forgive us more easily). The difference is in our timing and style. When the person asks for an answer and we immediately list ten good reasons for what we did, our explanation will be perceived as excusing or justifying our behavior. Instead, we want to think of how the other person must feel. He or she wants to know that we have taken clear responsibility for our acts and are truly sorry for the pain we caused. Once he or she believes those, he or she is open to understanding some of our reasons. After admitting his wrongdoing, George might say, "Would it help you to forgive me to know what was going on with me?"

OFFER YOUR REASONS WITHOUT BLAMING YOUR PARTNER

If the other person says, "Yes, I'd like to understand your reasons," then we can offer those reasons without suggesting that the other person made us hurt him or her.

Kisha says, "I'm truly sorry I poured ice water on you when you were sleeping. Would you like to know why?"

Lou says, "Yes, I would."

Kisha says, "I did it because you were being such a jerk to me that I couldn't respond any other way." Translation: You made me do it.

Needless to say, Kisha and Lou are going to spend the night in separate bedrooms dreaming about ice water. Kisha blamed Lou for her bad behavior. That will harden Lou's attitude and undo any positive gains that they might have made.

When Lou asked Kisha what her reasons were for dousing him in ice water, she probably should have said, "I was angry and I lost my temper." If she stays away from blaming Lou, they might still end up in different beds, but maybe they'll each dream less of ice water.

It's Time to REACH for Forgiveness

HOW TO BUY A LITTLE TIME

After one person makes the good CONFESSion, the ball bounces to the other side of the net. The other person will be forced to consider forgiving. Forgiveness is a gift, not a requirement. A grudging, surly "Sure I forgive you" with all the nonverbal signs of hatred will weaken, not strengthen, trust.

A grudging, surly "Sure I forgive you" with all the nonverbal signs of hatred will weaken, not strengthen, trust.

In our studies of forgiving, we found that every event is different. Sometimes we forgive shocking injustices in minutes or hours. Sometimes we nurse a grudge for years about the tiniest slights. But on the average, the longer we spend thinking empathically about the hurt, the more forgiveness we feel. When a friend stretches out her hand with a sincere request for forgiveness, we might rush up the Pyramid to REACH Forgiveness. But chances are, we'll need time to walk through the steps.

That creates a problem. When a person has made a good CONFESSion, that person has made himself or herself vulnerable. If we do not empathically respect that vulnerability, we can derail the rebuilding of trust. So we might say, "I really appreciate your admitting that you know you did wrong. It means a lot to me. I know how hard it is for me to say that I made a mistake, so I appreciate your sincere words and feelings. I want us to get past this event. I want to be able to forgive you. Even now I feel some forgiveness because I can see what you've gone through. I know the cost of confessing. For complete forgiveness, though, it's going to take some time. I'm trying hard to empathize and forgive you, but it might take me a while. Can you accept my appreciation for your apology and give me some time to work through these hard feelings?"

When we're alone, we can walk in a more leisurely way up the Pyramid. We can recall the hurt objectively, empathize with the person, consider times when we've been forgiven, and perhaps grant the altruistic gift of forgiveness.

If we've been asked for forgiveness, our public commitment to forgive (remember the C step of REACH) can be to tell the person that we have forgiven him or her. We might say, "Last week, you asked if I could forgive you for forgetting to come to my retirement party. I really appreciated your willingness to ask. I know that was hard. All week I thought about it. I do feel complete forgiveness. I wish I could have expressed it to you before now. Thank you for being willing to patch up our relationship."

In the same way that there is nothing magical about the mere words "I'm sorry," there is also nothing magical about the mere words "I forgive you." What we say is always qualified by how we say it and by the situation. Sometimes people use "I forgive you" as a way to stop conversation and make the other person feel guilty. They fold their arms, scowl, and mumble, "I forgive you."

Not surprisingly, when we're on the receiving end of such a communication, we don't feel forgiven. Yet if we say so, the other person says, "Why can't you let this drop? Why can't you take what I say at face value?" We are shamed by our attempts to reconcile; we feel that the conversation has been cut off. We have been put in a double bind.

In this case, we must be careful not to accuse the other person of negative intentions. Assume (whether you think it's true or not) that the other person wants to repair the relationship. Say, "I see that you care about our relationship. Thank you for forgiving me." By accepting the forgiveness as genuine, you allow the healing to progress. If you simply must confront the mixed message, say, "You say that you forgive me. But your face and body language seem to be giving me a different message. Chances are, I'm misreading your expression. I needed to check—for my peace of mind. I want to understand you. Can you help?"

FORGIVING LEADS TO RECONCILING

When people forgive, it often helps promote reconciliation. In South Africa's Truth and Reconciliation amnesty hearings, two men applied for amnesty for the murder of a local chief. The chief had been a despot, favorable to (and favored by) the apartheid regime. He had had many of his own people killed for petty reasons. The two men kidnapped and later murdered the chief. The amnesty hearings occasioned much public attention. As testimonies were winding down, one of the commissioners asked, "Does anyone else want to testify?"

A young man raised his hand. Immediately the room was abuzz with whispers. It was the chief's son. The potential for destruction of the reconciliation process was great. What if he denounced the hearing? What if he called for revolt against the process? The commissioners, committed to hearing the truth, allowed the young man to testify.

He addressed the murderers, saying something like, "When these hearings began, I wanted to see you both dead. But as I have heard about the horrible things that my father did to our people, I have changed. I wonder whether you could see it in your heart to forgive my family on behalf of what our father did. And also, if you would like to ask for our family's forgiveness for murdering our father, we would be glad to grant it." Instead of the violence that could have occurred if the young man had incited hate, reconciliation was furthered.

Forgiveness is like the sound of a waterfall after a long hike through the mountains. The dry hiking—placing one foot after another, sweating, straining—finally gives way to a splashing, cool waterfall. Yes, there is still a long hike to come, but forgiveness lets us look forward to the top, not down at the dusty trail.

Reconciliation is finally soaking your feet in the pool on top of the mountain. It is drinking cool, clear water, having a sweet, juicy apple, and enjoying the view.

Forgiveness can help promote reconciliation because it softens attitudes. If mutual forgiveness occurs, this is especially true.

Soft Talk and Hard Acts of Reconciliation

To promote reconciliation, we need soft talk about the hurt. To move beyond the Pyramid to REACH Forgiveness, people need to come to three agreements. They need not spell out every word, but they must reach a tacit agreement.

CAN WE AGREE TO FOCUS ON CHANGING OUR OWN BEHAVIOR, NOT THE OTHER PERSON'S?

Reconciliation is restoring trust through mutually trustworthy behavior. We naturally want to hold the other person accountable for his or her behavior. The other person's mistakes are easy to see, and almost easier to point out. Failures in trustworthiness are taken as evidence that the other person is either unwilling or unable to act trustworthily.

Yet focusing on the other person's behavior will not further the reconciliation nearly as fast nor as well as focusing on being trustworthy ourselves. Of course, that's the hard part. I know that I try hard yet often fall flat. I cut myself some slack when I blow it. I need to cut the other person some slack too. Even more, I need to focus on my own behavior.

> *Yet focusing on the other person's behavior will not further the reconciliation nearly as fast nor as well as focusing on being trustworthy ourselves.*

When I say that we naturally focus on the other person's negative acts, I'm speaking of the way we secretly feel about the cause of our relational woes. Some people are very direct with their blame. They criticize. They vocalize. They cut the other person down to size. Others blame themselves for relational problems. They feel victimized, and that feeling focuses their attention on their own inadequacies. They are ulcer getters, not ulcer givers. They focus on their own failures and inadequacies. When I recommend that we focus on our own behavior, I don't mean focus on our inadequacies. I mean focus on *changing* our behavior.

Both parties need to explicitly and implicitly agree that they will try to act trustworthily. Each needs to focus on himself or herself, not on keeping score for the other person.

Can We Agree on a Truce?

If reconciliation is to take place, hostilities need to cease. A truce should be explicitly agreed upon. A truce has two parts. One part is not acting in a hostile manner toward the other person. The other part is overlooking the other person's minor violations of the truce.

Let's illustrate a truce from a Chinese-American family in which an adolescent daughter was at war with her father. Monica bridled against her father's strict control. "My father is still living as if he was in Taiwan," she told her friends. "He's been in the United States more than twenty years but can't make the adjustment." She was upset because Mr. Han had grounded her for the third time in one semester.

She complained also to her mother: "It's not like I'm into drugs or sex. I just missed a curfew—that's all! He interprets everything I do as dishonoring him. He's driving me to dishonor him even more."

Monica's mother became the truce broker. She talked privately with her husband and convinced him to listen to Monica while trying to refrain from correcting her. Their talk led to a truce. Mr. Han agreed to be slower to use grounding as a punishment if Monica would try exceptionally hard to show honor and not disrespect to her father. Mrs. Han was assigned the role of recognizing and commenting on Monica's attempts to honor her father and on Mr. Han's instances of conscious restraint. The truce allowed the hostilities to cool down.

In another example, after Stanley and Steven had a disagreement at work, their supervisor called both into her office and encouraged them to reconcile. Both did not feel conciliatory, but they agreed to a truce and, specifically, to try to overlook minor provocations by the other. That agreement restored some peace within the office.

Putting the two parts of the truce together involves not acting hostilely and overlooking minor truce violations. For example, if the Protestants and Catholics in Ireland sign a truce and a young Catholic child throws rocks at a Protestant child, that is not of sufficient magnitude for the truce to be invalidated. In the same way, partners must agree to overlook small violations of the truce. Give the other person the benefit of the doubt.

CAN WE AGREE ON A PLAN TO RESTORE THE RELATIONSHIP?

Stopping hostilities is not the same thing as rebuilding the relationship. If trust has been damaged, trust must be rebuilt. That requires halting the downward slide. If a relationship is tumbling downhill at dizzying speed and both partners put on the brakes, they cannot expect the relationship to suddenly, instantaneously stop and start rolling uphill. At first, the slide downhill might continue, but at a slower pace. Eventually the slide stops. For a brief while, things are motionless. Then the wheels begin to move, perhaps slipping a bit at first. At last they catch and the relationship moves uphill.

> *Stopping hostilities is not the same thing as rebuilding the relationship. If trust has been damaged, trust must be rebuilt.*

As we restore a relationship, we must be realistic. Despite our best intentions, we will almost certainly at times fail to maintain a truce. We will fail to progress toward reconciliation. We must therefore make a plan for how to deal with failure.

It's easy to lose hope when we do not see progress occurring as fast as we would like. Hang in there. If both people stay positive, the relationship will change. Trust will grow.

Besides arresting the downward descent, starting the relationship back uphill, and making a plan for dealing with failure, partners need to at least begin to rebuild a positive relationship by detoxifying the relationship and building devotion. These steps are the last planks of the Bridge to Reconciliation.

CHAPTER 9

✳

Detoxification

Forgiveness, as an act of love, is felt, not achieved. It can be given, but it may not always be received. It cannot be bestowed as either a triumph over another person, or as the means to secure their humiliation or acquiescence. It is most healing, most profound, when it grows out of humility and realism, a hard-won sense that, whether you are entirely to blame in these events and I am blameless, there is in each of us insufficiencies and imperfections that can be our greatest teachers.

—STEPHANIE DOURICK

It was a beautiful gold pocket watch, passed down through three generations. When the top was clicked open, the face still gleamed white with black numerals. It kept excellent time. The problem with the watch from Hans's point of view was that it rested on Johann's mantel.

The watch was more a symbol of the Kruger family history than it was a valuable timepiece. Both Hans and Johann recalled the many stories their grandfather had told about coming to the United States with that watch in his pocket. When Grandfather had passed away, the stories were retold by Hans and Johann's father. Now he too had passed away.

TWO-SIDED TRANSGRESSIONS

Hans, the older brother, by rights should have had that watch. He was in line to inherit it, and the fact that his father hadn't mentioned the watch in the will was irrelevant. Johann shouldn't have gotten the watch. Yet Johann had anticipated the uncertainty and had gone into the house at night, before his father was even buried, and taken the watch. Now the watch mocked Hans from Johann's mantel.

After the funeral, the brothers argued bitterly about the watch. They shouted. They swore. Hans went to Johann's house that night and continued the argument. When Johann asked Hans to leave, Hans slipped the watch into his pocket and walked out with it. Before he got out of the driveway, Johann gave chase, but Hans sped off. Johann called the police and reported that Hans had stolen the watch. The police came to Hans's house, arrested him, and took him to the police station. He returned the watch with the understanding that Johann wouldn't prosecute him.

The War of the Watch wasn't over. Hans threatened to take the matter to court. He vowed to press his claim as the rightful owner of the watch and charge Johann with violating the estate prior to probate.

UNYIELDING UNFORGIVENESS

As the lawyers' fees mounted, Johann and Hans both became angrier and more bitter. The cost became so oppressive that Hans dropped the issue rather than continue to pour money into legal fees.

An uncomfortable truce settled in. For twenty years, neither brother visited the other. Neither acknowledged the other's existence. Although they lived less than two miles apart, they never spoke. When they met in the neighborhood or at the local supermarket, they simply walked past each other.

PLANK 1: DECISIONS (POSSIBILITIES OF RECONCILIATION EMERGE)

Maybe the uneasy truce in the War of the Watch would have lasted for the rest of their lives had not their children met in college. As amazing as it seems, the two cousins, living two miles apart, had never met before they had a course together at the large state university. Annamarie had heard her father, Johann, talk many times about Hans's stealing the watch from Johann's mantel. Fred had heard often about Johann's nighttime raid before their father's body was laid to rest. Never having met, Annamarie and Fred were not as emotionally invested in the conflict as were their fathers. They struck up a conversation and became fast friends during the semester.

When Annamarie brought up her budding friendship with Fred, Johann forbade her to see Fred anymore. Annamarie wanted to honor her father, but Fred sat near her in class. They continued to talk. Perhaps Annamarie was going through a rebellious time, or perhaps she simply didn't want to carry on the family feud. For whatever reason, Fred and she became even closer. Near the end of the semester, Annamarie talked with her father again. She was forthright in admitting that she had continued to talk with Fred. At first Johann was furious. As she talked more about Fred's positive qualities, though, Johann grudgingly admitted that he seemed to share some of Hans's good traits.

Shortly after that, Hans bumped into Johann as they stood in line to renew their driver's licenses. Both felt trapped, but waiting in long lines seems part of the shared experience of modern humanity. Johann mentioned the class that Annamarie and Fred shared. To his surprise, Hans responded. It was their first talk in twenty years. Both avoided any reference to the War of the Watch.

As they neared the front of the line, one of the brothers mentioned that they had waited for a long time. The mere mention of time triggered bad memories. Their conversation petered out after some harsh words, then lapsed into silence.

That night when Johann described the incident to his wife, he recounted several criticisms that Hans had levied against him. Johann's daughter, Annamarie, overheard and asked Johann directly whether the criticisms were true. Johann pondered the question longer than he had intended and hesitatingly admitted that there was some truth to some of them. Admitting that to his daughter made him reconsider things he had said against Hans. He wasn't proud of his constant criticism. So he determined to stop criticizing Hans so much to his family. For several weeks, he did not make one critical statement, despite Annamarie's continuing to talk about her friendship with Fred.

PLANK 2: DISCUSSION

Johann wanted the war to be over. On an impulse one night, he called Hans and asked if they could get together on neutral ground. They met for dinner at a local steakhouse. To Johann's surprise, they had a pleasant time during the evening. Two weeks later, Hans called Johann to arrange lunch. Their second meeting again turned out fine, and their boyhood friendship began to be rekindled.

Johann decided to take the plunge. He invited Hans to his home for dinner. Hans accepted. The evening went well until, near the end, Hans insulted Johann. Each family member waited for the explosion. Johann, after a pause, continued the conversation as if the insult hadn't happened. Everyone exhaled.

Over time, Johann and Hans met regularly. Their relationship grew strong again. But Johann still had the watch.

Three years after the relationship between Johann and Hans began to mend, Fred graduated from college. Johann and Annamarie together gave him a graduation present—his great-grandfather's watch. Fred was flabbergasted. He turned to Annamarie, who said, "Dad and I did this together. I have no use for a watch, and we thought it should be passed to a man within our family." She reached inside the collar of her blouse and looped her finger around the chain that had always hung from the watch, now made into a necklace. "Now we both have a memento of our heritage," she said.

Hans and Johann stood by, watching the reconciliation of the families. Johann faced Hans and said, "Brother, I was wrong to have taken the watch from the house. Can you ever forgive me?"

They hugged. "No problem. It wasn't all one-sided," said Hans. "I tried to steal it back, and that was wrong too. Can you forgive me?"

"Long ago," said Johann, and gave Hans another big bear hug.

The Final Planks in the Bridge to Reconciliation

If you've considered whether, how, and when to reconcile (Plank 1, decisions) and talked with the other person about forgiveness (Plank 2, discussion), then the hard work of restoration of the relationship has begun in earnest. Now you have to do two more things. You must reverse the direction of the downhill slide of the relationship and remove the poison from the relationship (Plank 3, detoxification), and you must actively attempt to rebuild love into the relationship (Plank 4, devotion). I'll discuss detoxification in the present chapter and devotion in the final chapter. First, let's tackle the hard job—looking honestly into the mirror, not just to see our acts, as we have done before, but to see into our hearts.

Following the Hard Way

BLOOD ON THE CARPET

When treasured trust has been violated and bad blood exists between us and another person, we usually want to restore trust if we can. We long to detoxify that bad blood. If only we could run the bad blood of both parties through relationship dialysis! If only we could remove the vile poisons from our interactions! Unfortunately, it's not just the poison in the other person's heart, or even the poison in our relationship, that needs detoxification. Sometimes there's poison in our own soul as well.

I grew up in the house in which my mother was murdered. I lived at home for twenty-two years. After I moved away, I visited several times a year. When my children were in high school, we walked the roads I walked when I was growing up. I shared with them my memories of boyhood adventures.

Right after the murder, I went back to the house several times. We toured the house with police officers. They were trying to learn what might have been stolen during the burglary. We entered through the back door. The broken windowpane, which had been used for the initial entry, was boarded shut. Secure, but too late.

Stepping through the back door into the kitchen, I felt that I had been transported into the remnant of an earthquake. The toaster had been thrown through the microwave. The refrigerator had been pulled away from the wall. Black fingerprint dust smeared its front and side. Palm prints stood out, smudged with dust. Debris was scattered across the kitchen. We picked our way through cracked dishes, pots, pans, canisters sitting askew on cones of flour. The search for money and valuables had been as violent as it was violating.

As I stepped into the hallway, I looked down the hall at the gray carpet. My eyes were drawn to two pools of still-gooey blood at the end of the hall, and the blood splattered along the walls and on the bedroom door. Each pool was the size of a kitchen plate traced with a trembling hand. One was where Mama's head would have lain, the other where her hips would have rested.

As I looked at those pools of blood, I thought, *At least she couldn't have suffered long. She didn't seem to have bled much before her heart stopped beating.* That was something of a comfort.

To get to every room in the main part of the house, we had to walk through the hallway. Each step back into the hall assaulted me with images of blood. Each assault was a gut shot.

I left with the scene of violence burned into my brain. In our culture, we have become almost numb to violence. We watch murders on television. We plunk down money to see slasher movies. We read novels about bloody killings without batting an eye. We see violence on the news.

I had been involved in some violence myself. In junior high school, I blundered into the bathroom just before a gang fight broke out. I saw one boy whipped with a chain while a gang stood around, threatening those of us in the bathroom who weren't involved in either gang.

I was playing basketball as a junior in high school when an opposing player suddenly threw the ball down and came after me, swinging his fists. I took a blow to the mouth. The ring on his finger cut my lip and cut my trumpet-playing days short at the same time. I was not a stranger to violence.

Yet seeing the inside of the house in which I grew up destroyed was a slam to the head. Seeing the dark blood of my mother, who poured out her life raising me, pooled on the carpet snapped my eyes wide open with a slap. The police officer said that the only valuables that seemed to be missing were a few dollars in loose change. That was another slap. The tragedy and the waste of violence hit home.

Later that week, I went back to our old house to meet the claims adjusters. While we talked amid the carnage, two men arrived. "We're here to replace the damaged carpet," said one. They sliced through the carpet about one yard from each side of the center of the two bloodstains. They tugged the carpet away from the floor. Underneath, there was a pool of sticky gore that was at least a yard in diameter.

I could feel my legs get shaky. The fragile illusion that I had held all week—that my mother had not suffered much after being bludgeoned—was ripped away with the carpet.

She must have lain there a long time as her heart pumped her lifeblood into those pools that ran underneath the carpet, I thought. The ugliness beneath was far wider than what showed on the surface of the carpet.

I thought that unforgiveness might rear up in me again. Instead I felt only a huge sense of sorrow for my mom's suffering. Strangely, I felt a new wave of compassion for the youth who committed the murder. It was clear that he *needed* forgiveness even more than I had originally thought. In my soul, I could only cry out to God that he might have mercifully spared my mother consciousness. I prayed for mercy on her murderer. The guilt of what he had done must be torturing him.

Detoxifying Our Soul

Seeing the blood beneath the carpet was one of the strongest, most persistent mental images I've ever had. Since that day, I have thought even more about forgiveness than ever before. Standing eye to eye with the horror, ugliness, and waste of murder changed me. I knew experientially how low we humans could descend. I also knew experientially how much we need forgiveness.

I have often spoken publicly about my mother's death. People have asked many times, "How can you possibly forgive?" Some people have suggested that I must have some special courage or character trait that helped me forgive.

I do not think so. I know my own heart. I know the struggles that I've gone through trying to forgive. I don't always succeed. In fact, I fail too often. I hold unforgiveness too long.

My students once hurt me by giving me lower teacher ratings than I wanted. I struggled for months to forgive them. In my moments of reflection, I had to admit to myself that whether I received super teacher ratings from every class wasn't very important among life's priorities. Faculty members have criticized some of my actions as chair of the Department of Psychology. I struggled for months to forgive them. A professional colleague criticized my character. I struggled for over a year to forgive that person. I have experienced rejections, betrayals, and slights—just as we all have. I have held on to some grudges for years.

Yet here is the miracle. When I had to forgive the most horrible, seemingly hard-to-forgive event—my mother's murder—I could do that within a day.

I am sad to say, from the point of view of my self-esteem, that it was not positive character that let me forgive quickly. In many ways, being able to forgive is a gift, or perhaps a mercy, that we don't necessarily deserve or work to earn. Sometimes we forgive because we initiate forgiveness. Sometimes we forgive because it just seems to happen to us. Sadly, sometimes we struggle and cannot forgive.

> *Sometimes we forgive because we initiate forgiveness. Sometimes we forgive because it just seems to happen to us. Sadly, sometimes we struggle and cannot forgive.*

I knew my character flaws and was all too aware of some of the petty unforgiveness that was beneath the surface. I saw the imperfections in my own heart that others cannot always see. My acts were similar to the blood *on* the carpet. My soul was like the blood *beneath* the carpet.

The toxic waste in our own soul can be far greater than what others see. Yet—and this is the hard news—it is that unseen toxicity that needs to be cleaned out before we can detoxify our relationships. Before I can begin to detoxify the unforgiveness within, I must be willing to admit that I am unforgiving. I have to look at my heart squarely and admit that I have a heart disease. I need to forgive from my heart.

FORGIVING MYSELF

We don't have to forgive ourselves *before* we can forgive a transgressor. Yet we must forgive ourselves *as well as* forgiving the transgressor if it's going to make much difference in our lives. Self-condemnation not only can make us miserable, but can also make it more difficult to restore our relationships.

We underestimate how hard it is to forgive ourselves. First, it's hard to admit that we've done wrong. I prefer to think of myself as someone who "makes mistakes" or "means well." Second, I don't like to think that I could plan to do wrong intentionally. I don't like to admit to negative motives. It's so hard to forgive myself for negative acts and motives, but with effort I can do it.

Forgiving my own transgressions is little different from forgiving someone else's. I can employ the REACH steps. Suppose I lost my temper and yelled at my administrative assistant. I should recall (R) the incident vividly. Also important: I should spend substantial time empathizing (E) with myself. Why did I lose my temper? I was under a lot of stress. My boss was pressing for a project immediately. I had been criticized by two colleagues earlier that morning. I got a speeding ticket the day before. My administrative assistant was particularly annoying. He refused to do a job I had assigned him, and when I returned from a meeting, he was on the computer playing solitaire. If I look deep within myself, I can see that I was not only reacting to his insolence, but envious of his relaxing while I was working. I probably, deep down, wanted to punish him for being relaxed. That's an ugly motive that I don't like to admit, but if I can see how the envy developed, I can perhaps forgive those darker motives.

By empathizing with myself, I treat myself with the same respect I treat others with. That might help me move through the A, C, and H steps of REACH and forgive myself for losing my temper.

When I get to this point, I usually think, *Ah, I've forgiven myself. I'm glad that's done.*

But usually it isn't done. I still feel self-condemnation.

As it turns out, forgiving our acts and even our motives is only part of forgiving ourselves. The harder part—the part we usually fail to consider—is that we cannot forgive ourselves for being *the type of person who could do the evil.* We can forgive our acts. We often cannot forgive our own character.

So I admit to myself: I did yell at my assistant. I did act out of envy. I have forgiven those. But I don't forgive myself for being the type of person who would do those things. My acts and motives weren't consistent with my self-image. Forgiving myself for tarnishing my self-image is difficult. How can I do that?

To forgive ourselves, we need to be forgiven. We need to find out that we are forgivable—that we are acceptable even with a halo that is slightly askew. Someone else needs to be able to forgive us. The kind of self-forgiveness that we can generate in ourselves by thinking that we must be forgivable is usually not enough to cleanse us. It can remove some spots, but it does no deep cleaning.

> *To forgive ourselves, we need to be forgiven. We need to find out that we are forgivable—that we are acceptable even with a halo that is slightly askew.*

For some people, we're all we have. Others have a loved one who can help us believe we are forgivable and therefore help us forgive ourselves. That loved one can help us admit the weaknesses of our character. He or she can encourage us to grant merciful forgiveness for what we did, and even more, for what we are. Still others turn to God or a higher power for forgiveness. Divine forgiveness can help them forgive themselves.

If you are struggling with self-condemnation, can you seek out someone you trust enough to talk with? If you need divine forgiveness, seek it. Even if you can find no listening ear, you can write to yourself in a journal. By talking about your painful character flaws with someone else, you are taking a big step—equivalent to the R and E steps to help you REACH forgiveness of yourself for your disappointment in your own character weaknesses.

As you see, forgiving yourself isn't easy. It is a continuing lifetime work. We all are imperfect and knock our halos askew regularly. Sometimes we seem to throw them in the mud and grind them beneath our heel. The hard truth is that we must pick up the dirty halo and look squarely at the mud. The halo won't spontaneously clean itself. We must courageously face our imperfect character.

When we're over the hump and have begun to forgive ourselves, or perhaps while we're still struggling, we cannot remain still. We must act if we are to rescue a relationship that is plunging downhill.

Reverse the Negative Slide

RELATIONSHIP RUPTURE

Unforgiveness is being trapped in a sudden squall—buffeted, battered, and beaten. It is fearing you will never escape or fearing that you will escape only to find yourself headed for the rocks, angry and resentful at the storm, bitter at your luck.

Suddenly, as abruptly as the squall began, it passes. You sail into sunshine. You forgive. Of course, there is damage still to repair—flapping sails to secure, water to pump from the bilge, loose sheets, wet charts, perhaps a malfunctioning guidance system and a wrecked radio. It isn't going to be easy to get home to safety and security. But the stark difference between the squall and the sunshine gives hope. And hope makes all the difference.

John Gottman, a psychologist at the University of Washington in Seattle, has studied marriages for thirty years.[1] He has shown that when marriages deteriorate, they usually do so in four predictable steps. I have found those steps to be just as true for friendships, work relationships, and parent-child relationships as for marriage.

The first step involves criticism. At first, people criticize each other in their mind, then the criticism becomes verbal. Second, defensiveness appears as the other person hears the criticisms. The defensiveness is initially mental, but over time, it becomes verbal. Criticism plus defensiveness equals arguments. The third step in relationship rupture is contempt. With contempt, each person changes his or her view of the relationship. Whereas criticism and defensiveness both tend to be specific to acts of the other person, contempt is directed at the person himself or herself. The fourth stage of relationship rupture is what Gottman calls "stonewalling." Each person who has been hurt many times throws up a potential stone wall. As Simon and Garfunkel said, "A rock feels no pain." Each person's attitude is "You can't get to me. Whatever you say will bounce off just as if it had struck a stone wall."

Straws and Camels' Backs

A direct connection seems to exist between being positive and feeling happy with the relationship. Gottman found, however, that as he observed married couples precisely, dramatic differences in their relationship were likely, depending on a couple's ratio of positive to negative interactions. If one couple had ten, seven, or even five times as many positive interactions as negative ones, they were usually very happy. But when couples had a ratio of positive to negative interactions below five to one, it usually was not four to one. Instead it was one to one or one to two.

At five to one, an abrupt transformation occurred, as if a rope had snapped. People above the five-to-one break generally saw the relationship positively. People below the break saw mostly the negative.

When good families or friendships turn sour, they usually erode slowly—like marriages. In a relationship on the edge, one negative event can push the people over the threshold to a negative, pain-filled relationship. At some point, a threshold might be reached. The straw breaks the camel's back. It's as if the two people whip off their rose-colored glasses and slam on dark glasses. Through those, they can see only the negative in each other and the relationship. They develop contempt for the other *person*, not just the other person's behavior. The relationship can quickly degenerate to where each person divorces himself or herself from feelings and turns into a stone wall. Only a dramatic turnaround can prevent the rupture.

> *At some point, a threshold might be reached. The straw breaks the camel's back. It's as if the two people whip off their rose-colored glasses and slam on dark glasses. Through those, they can see only the negative in each other and the relationship.*

In a positive relationship, people might be unforgiving toward each other, although usually small hurts are either forgiven, quickly forgotten, or forborne. But if the relationship slides into troubled waters, partners find that it becomes harder to overlook the negative. They ruminate about the negative. Rumination is, of course, at the core of unforgiveness. The relationship fills with resentment, bitterness, perhaps even hatred.

RECONCILIATION REQUIRES DETOXIFICATION
OF RELATIONSHIP POISONS

When a relationship has gone bad, usually increasing doses of poison have been injected through toxic interactions. Finally, a critical level of toxins makes the relationship sick.

To reconcile, we must reverse the buildup of relationship poison as we climb stepwise from stonewalling to contempt to defensiveness to criticism. Then we must move further so that infrequent criticism is again the norm. At some point as we forgive and claw our way inch by inch out of our relationship sickness, a sudden transformation usually occurs. One day the relationship looks rocky; the next, the way is paved. We find our rose-colored glasses. They might have some smudges on the lenses, but they let in a lot more light than the dark glasses.

When we are reconciling, we must assess our relationship to determine whether it has deteriorated through those four stages that Gottman identified. If we find our relationship is in one of the stages of deterioration, we need to detoxify our communication before it can move to a higher stage. While we would all prefer instant, total relationship detoxification, usually we must settle for moving back up the cascade step by step.

MOVE FROM STONEWALLING BACK TO CONTEMPT

For example, if we have gotten to the stage of stonewalling, in which we have deadened our feelings toward the other person, then we must first try to recover our feeling. We must decide whether to risk having a serious discussion with each other or someone else about the relationship. If so, we must commit ourselves not to hurt the other person during the discussion. We can adopt a cease-fire and attempt to have a positive discussion. If we are successful, we can at least get back into contact with each other.

Obviously, we must protect ourselves from harm during a discussion. We know that if we don't do anything differently, the relationship will move past stonewalling to a parting of the ways.

To detoxify, it's helpful to consider what would be lost if the relationship crumbles. Will parents lose contact with their children? Will long-married couples lose years of shared good memories? Will business partners lose financial stability? Will friends lose pleasant relations with each other? The goal for each person should be to reengage.

By feeling again, we take a risk. We risk being hurt. But by risking, we might have our relationship restored.

We might get angry with each other, feel pain, feel frustration. Of course, no one likes to feel those negative feelings. Despite this, if we're attempting to scale stonewalling hearts, then feeling anger and pain is actually a positive step. Pain indicates that we still have some feeling for each other.

Rudy and Dorrie sat in my counseling office. Their closed postures reflected their closed hearts toward each other. At the beginning of the eight weeks of counseling they had agreed to, they weren't interested in repairing their marriage. They were looking for a validation of their incompatibility that could be traded for a low-guilt divorce.

Then Rudy went away to a business conference and attended a seminar on business communication. On the flight home, he reached a decision, which he dropped like a bomb into counseling.

"I realized that my life was like a bunch of refrigerators. Our marriage was cooling in one compartment. My passion for my job was freezing in another compartment. I don't even like to watch television anymore. I don't want to live this way."

Dorrie faced Rudy for the first time all hour. "I think that's the most vulnerable statement I've ever heard you make." Her compliment was mixed with criticism, but fortunately Rudy responded to the compliment, not the criticism.

"I want us to get our marriage out of the cooler. I'm worried that if we do, we'll fight. But anything is better than being on a slab in a morguelike refrigerator."

Dorrie began to cry.

Rudy and Dorrie were far from being happily married, but they had at least moved back into the land of the living. Rudy's measured vulnerability started their conversation. Dorrie's vulnerability kept them talking. For a while they were able to express themselves instead of living walled-off refrigerator lives.

At this point, a quick granting of forgiveness that doesn't touch the heart would have been merely a cold forgiveness. Surface forgiveness can be one more stone in the stone wall. Surface forgiveness often comes from a snow-covered heart. Warmhearted forgiveness is different.

MOVE FROM CONTEMPT BACK TO DEFENSIVENESS

If the relationship hasn't deteriorated all the way to stonewalling but is in the stage of contempt, then we generally feel that the other person's character flaws are causing the problem. We must move away from this belief if reconciliation is to occur.

We should recall the good things that the other person has done. We tell ourselves that those acts are just as much a part of the other person's character as are the flaws. We must realize that when we're upset, we see more flaws than strengths in the other person or in the relationship. It's helpful (but hard) for us to remind ourselves that we're not perfect either.

Hector and Jennifer seemed to loathe each other. Their contempt dripped from every evaluation of the other. They were headed for divorce.

Ironically, it was country line dancing that got them back together. Jennifer had been going to a community center to dance with her friends. Hector despised dancing. Then Hector's best friend Julio and his wife started going dancing. They invited Hector and, in a "moment of weakness," as he later described it, he agreed to go.

In spite of his prejudice against dancing, he got hooked. Then he and Jennifer began to drive to the dances together. The big change happened in Hector. He realized that if he could be so wrong in his contempt for line dancing, then maybe he was wrong about some of Jennifer's other habits and personal qualities as well. That mundane opening moved them into serious conversation. Talk and shared fun helped them repair some of the damage to their marriage.

It might be helpful to recall the words of Aleksandr Solzhenitsyn, who said, "If only there were evil people somewhere insidiously committing evil deeds, and it were necessary only to separate them from the rest of us and destroy them. But the line dividing good and evil cuts through the heart of every human being. And who is willing to destroy a piece of his own heart?" A related quote is by Thomas à Kempis: "Be not angry that you cannot make others as you wish them to be, since you cannot make yourself as you wish you to be."

Move from Defensiveness Back to Criticism

If we find ourselves in the stage of relationship rupture in which we are extremely defensive, we will often snap back into a negative mind-set the instant we believe the person is criticizing us. To reconcile, we first need to recognize how our defensiveness gets in our way.

How defensive are you? Take the Defensiveness Self-Test opposite. If you score 15 to 30, you are very defensive.

Once you recognize how defensive and reactive you are, you need to defuse yourself. Instead of snapping back into negativity or snapping back at the other person, you can soothe your anger by taking a few deep breaths. Deep breathing calms the body by activating the parasympathetic nervous system, which calms us. Once you're calm, you're ready to examine the criticism to which you're having this knee-jerk reaction. If you think there's any truth to it, admit that truth to yourself and try not to provoke the other person.

There is no one right way to react to every criticism, but I have found through my own mistakes that there are many ways that are always unhelpful. If I go blind with rage and blast the person who criticizes me, I will almost always pay a price later that is out of proportion to the relief I got from exploding. If I criticize the other person in return, it usually leads to escalating hostility. If I bear a grudge and punish the person later, it not only hurts my relationship with the person, but damages my own integrity.

> *If I go blind with rage and blast the person who criticizes me, I will almost always pay a price later that is out of proportion to the relief I got from exploding.*

When I am criticized—and, as anyone in a leadership position knows, criticism is frequent and often viciously personal—I try to ask myself what my goals are for the relationship. Do I want to mend damages? Or do I want the relief of emotional catharsis regardless of the consequences?

Most of the time, I decide to stifle my defensiveness and stay calm. Most of the time, reconciliation takes precedence over my wounded ego.

How Defensive Are You?

Defensiveness Self-Test

As you ponder a particular relationship, answer these questions.

Circle the one that applies

1. Do you feel misunder-   Often   Sometimes   Never
   stood by the other person?

2. Do you have silent   Often   Sometimes   Never
   arguments in your head
   with the other person?

3. Do you wake up in the   Often   Sometimes   Never
   middle of the night unable
   to get back to sleep because
   of the silent arguments
   with the other person?

4. Do you feel criticized   Often   Sometimes   Never
   by the other person?

5. Do you feel that the   Often   Sometimes   Never
   other person is violating
   your basic rights?

6. Do you feel angry at   Often   Sometimes   Never
   the other person?

7. Do you argue with the   Often   Sometimes   Never
   other person?

8. Do you feel that you   Often   Sometimes   Never
   never get the last word
   when you talk to the
   other person?

9. Do you feel attacked   Often   Sometimes   Never
   by the other person?

continued

Circle the one that applies

10. Do you feel sorry because Often Sometimes Never
you have acted negatively
toward the other person?

HOW TO SCORE YOUR DEFENSIVENESS SELF-TEST

Total the number of times you circled "Often" and multiply by 2. Put your answer here.

_____

Total the number of times you circled "Sometimes" and put that total here.

_____

Add the two and put the sum here. This is your defensiveness score.

_____

If your defensiveness score is:

15–30	You are highly defensive
6–14	You are somewhat defensive
0–5	You are not defensive

For instance, I offended a faculty member in my department by not recognizing the contributions she made to arranging a large public lecture. She confronted me. My mind swirled with justifications, but deep down, I knew she was right. I swallowed my ego and didn't lash back by bringing up times when she had dishonored me. I publicly apologized to her.

Of course, sometimes we are accused of wrongdoing and we

know we did no wrong. One of my daughters, Becca, wanted me to attend a school play she was in. I told her I would come. A freak spring snowstorm hit the Shenandoah Mountains and the Highway Patrol closed the interstate over the mountain, which prevented me from getting to her play. Naturally, Becca was disappointed and hurt that I couldn't come. When I talked with her, I was able to acknowledge that I had hurt her and apologize even though I realized that I hadn't done anything wrong.

Move from Criticism Back to Normalcy

Criticizing others is a tough habit to break. It's easier if we focus on the other person's good qualities instead of his or her negative, aggravating qualities. Or we can consider what pressures the person might be under. We can try to discern what is pushing the other person to act in ways that we find aggravating. Then we can try to ease some of those pressures to help the person be less stressed. In the best case, it's helpful to think about what we might have done to incite the person to act negatively. If you discover some provocation, apologize for what you did.

If you're like me, you probably read the last two paragraphs and nodded. You might have even thought, *Sure, that sounds like a great idea. Think of the positive. Try to figure out what's going on behind the scenes.* But you won't succeed unless you actually make this intention concrete. I tell the people in my workshop to make a list of the other person's good qualities and pressures on him or her. It's hard not to feel empathy when you're looking at a list in black and white.

Yesterday, I had a small confrontation at work. It wasn't the first with this person. I realized that I would have flunked the defensiveness test if I had taken it (which I didn't). I had been very critical. So I took my own advice. I actually made a list of the person's positive qualities. I considered the pressures the person was under. I (gulp) even examined my own behavior and realized I needed to apologize, which I did via e-mail. The person acknowledged my e-mail, and our relationship took a giant step toward reconciliation.

So instead of reading quickly through these steps, apply them. Is a relationship at work going sour? Make a list of the person's positive qualities. Is a parent-child relationship more negative than you want? Examine your own behavior.

REVISITING THE WAR OF THE WATCH

In the War of the Watch, we saw Johann and Hans's relationship deteriorate. They accumulated negative events and violations of trust until the relationship slid off the precipice. They criticized each other and reacted defensively toward each other. Each felt nothing but contempt for the other. Johann was contemptuous of Hans for stealing the watch from his mantel. Hans was contemptuous of Johann for stealing the watch from their father's house before the father was even buried. They each turned into stone walls.

Through their children's relationship, Johann began to move toward reconciliation. His stone wall was chipped away when Annamarie told him about her growing acquaintance with Fred, Hans's son. Johann reacted in anger, but at least he was feeling. Johann and Hans met with each other and talked. Even though anger flared up at the end, they at least moved beyond their earlier contempt for each other. When Annamarie questioned whether the criticisms levied by Hans against Johann were true, instead of reacting defensively, Johann actually considered them. He began seriously to consider acting differently toward Hans. Both Johann and Hans moved beyond criticism by meeting twice on neutral ground. By the time that Johann invited Hans to his home for dinner, they had both begun to walk across the Bridge to Reconciliation. They had begun to detoxify their relationship. Next, they needed to detoxify their expectations.

Detoxifying Negative Expectations

Reconciliation involves restoring damaged trust. But what if the other person does something that violates our trust again? Even a small infraction is a fresh violation of trust. What should we do? Should we give up and write off the effort to reconcile as doomed to failure because the other person is flawed beyond redemption? Or can we plan a more positive way to manage failures in trustworthiness?

> *Reconciliation involves restoring damaged trust. But what if the other person does something that violates our trust again?*

When people have developed a history of hurts and offenses, those wounds often lie just beneath the skin, apparently healed over, but tender to the touch. They can be reopened at the slightest provocation. Expectations are still poisoned.

AN EXAMPLE OF POISONED EXPECTATIONS

William Faulkner in *Requiem for a Nun* said, "The past is not dead; it's not even past." This truth is nowhere more evident than responses to the Holocaust. Jews and non-Jews alike are committed to remembering the evil that humans are capable of and have perpetrated against other humans.

In fact, such human rights violations still occur on a large scale throughout the world, even today. We know of the horrors in places such as Cambodia, Sierra Leone, Rwanda, Laos, Sudan, Guatemala, Chile, Bosnia, and Kosovo. In each conflict, each side tells its own history. In Rwanda, the Hutus and Tutsis teach their separate histories to their children. Is it a mystery what will happen when this generation of children, with their separate histories, become adults? Armed with separate blame-splattered histories, each side will be primed for new bloodletting.

Despite the almost worldwide sense of guilt over the Holocaust, there is always the danger that such events will become "simply history." If we forget or minimize the Holocaust, the moral and emotional power that might prevent such atrocities from recurring will be lost. Yet our remembering sometimes causes us to expect the worst.

This necessary tension was dramatized on the world stage in 1985. In the beginning scene of the first act, the chancellor of West Germany, Helmut Kohl, invited President Ronald Reagan to come to Germany to participate in the fortieth anniversary of the end of the war in Europe. The ceremony was intended to be a sign of reconciliation between the United States and Germany. In the ensuing four months, President Reagan responded to the invitation. He announced that he would participate in the reconciliation ceremony but would not visit a concentration camp because it might reawaken old memories and stir up the always-simmering pain from the Holocaust.

Reagan's announcement was criticized by Jews and non-Jews alike. People demanded to know why the president didn't want to visit the concentration camp. Behind this denunciation seemed to lurk a fear that the Holocaust would be first officially (and later privately) forgotten. Critics were upset that soldiers of Germany would be honored, but not the (Jewish) victims of Germany.

On April 16, 1985, President Reagan announced that he

would visit a graveyard in Bitburg to honor the German dead there. He portrayed the dead in that cemetery, though they were Germans, as victims of Nazism, just as the Jews had been victims of Nazism. He did not realize that there were forty-nine SS soldiers buried in that cemetery. Critics accused Reagan not just of trying to sweep the Holocaust under the rug, but also of honoring some of its worst perpetrators.

On April 19, 1985, Nobel Peace Prize winner Elie Wiesel, a survivor of a prison camp, was slated to receive the Congressional Gold Medal, the highest honor that Congress bestows on a civilian. Wiesel gave an impassioned speech aimed directly at Reagan. Wiesel argued that Reagan's moral commitment should be to the victims of the SS and not to SS perpetrators of crimes against humanity. Wiesel described scenes that he had seen as a prisoner at Auschwitz. He argued that the issue was not about politics, but about good versus evil. Wiesel acknowledged that President Reagan was seeking to restore relations between the United States and the German people. He said that he didn't believe in collective guilt or collective responsibility. Rather, he held the killers (i.e., the SS) responsible for their acts. Wiesel criticized Reagan's lack of sensitivity to the victims of the Holocaust. Reagan admitted that he was moved by Wiesel's passion. Yet he did not cancel his visit to Bitburg.

In both Germany and the United States, public opinion crystallized around this issue. In the Senate, a scant majority of senators condemned Reagan's decision. Public polls on the issue in the United States were divided. By the end of this episode, when Reagan finally laid the wreath at Bitburg, a number of leaders, both in the United States and in Germany, had made public statements about reconciliation and about the necessity of remembering the evil that had been done in the Holocaust. At Bitburg,

Reagan said, "Many of you are worried that reconciliation means forgetting. I promise you, we will never forget." He went on, "We celebrate today the reconciliation between our two nations that has liberated us from that cycle of destruction."

The experience at Bitburg conveys graphically that hurts do not magically go away simply because they are past. Certainly, the Holocaust is worthy of our memory. *How* we remember makes all the difference. Memories can be brought up with a venom betraying bitter unforgiveness, in a spirit of righteous and haughty indignation, or in a spirit of firm but well-meaning confrontation, as with Wiesel's confrontation of Reagan. Traumatic and emotion-laden memories pop unbidden into our minds. They can push us quickly back into ruminating, unforgiveness, the telling stories in which we are victims of harm or prejudice. We cannot stop the traumatic and emotional memories from arising. But we can derail the negativity before it gets up a head of steam if we detoxify our thoughts, expectations, and speech.

EVIDENCE OF THE NEED TO DETOXIFY

Memories of past transgressions arise when we experience a new (similar) hurt, when we are under stress, or when we are reminded of the old transgression. Merely remembering an old wound is not a sign that we need to detoxify our relationship. How do we know if we need to do this? There are some telltale signs: We (1) reproach the transgressor by bringing up past hurts instead of merely dealing with the current hurt, (2) make an overly harsh reproach, (3) attack the other person rather than sticking to the issue, (4) hear bitterness in our voice, or (5) cannot let go of a past hurt.

When we see the need to detoxify our mutual bitterness and

resentment, the issue is usually not merely one of forgiveness but one of reconciliation as well. That is, we need to restore trust.

The most common sign of the need to detoxify that I see in my workshops is the urge to unload emotional memories of hurt and betrayal. If you unload a litany of past betrayals, it's called "kitchen-sinking" because you hit the transgressor with everything but the kitchen sink. The transgressor is flooded with too many issues to deal with. If you catch yourself kitchen-sinking, stop and deal with the single current violation of trust. The two of you can more likely work out an understanding and rebuild trust if you deal with one issue at a time until it's resolved.

DEVELOPING HELPFUL EXPECTANCIES

If we want to reconcile with someone, we need some plan for dealing with failures in trustworthiness. Such failures are almost inevitable. Once our trust has been broken, we're often sensitized to look for violations in trustworthiness. We might perceive betrayals where objectively none exists. The other person is usually just as sensitized and often thinks we've broken trust at the slightest opportunity.

When we think that the other person hasn't been trustworthy, we're often quick to conclude that reconciliation has failed. The other person's lack of perfection is taken as proof positive that he or she never intended to change, was unable to change, was unwilling to change, and could not ever be trusted to change.

If reconciliation is to succeed, we must see failures in trustworthiness as not only unsurprising, but expected. This attitude is hard to maintain. We might admit that, theoretically, we are not trustworthy 100 percent of the time, but if we mess up, we cut ourselves huge amounts of slack. When we notice our own betrayals of trust, we are clearly aware of the pressures and good reasons that forced us to behave as we did. We have a hard time understanding the pressures on the other person. We take the other person's failures as proof of a persistently negative personality.

> *If reconciliation is to succeed, we must see failures in trustworthiness as not only unsurprising, but expected.*

Instead of being thrown by failures in trustworthiness—either our own or the other person's—we should think of these failures as opportunities to practice forgiveness. Theologian Henri J. M. Nouwen said, "Forgiveness is love practiced among people who love poorly." See the other person's failures in trustworthiness as opportunities to build your forgiving-personality disposition. See your own failures as opportunities to practice humility. When transgressions rip apart relationships, forgiveness is the seamstress who reweaves the jagged tear in trust thread by thread. Forgiveness restores the raveled seam of love and irons out the wrinkles of residual anger.

ATTITUDES OF LATITUDE AND GRATITUDE

The process of reconciliation is one step backward and two steps forward. In our fantasies, progress is continuous and rapid, but in real life, progress is herky-jerky. When reconciliation takes one step backward, we should try to practice an "attitude of latitude." We try to tolerate the other person's imperfections and failures because we are aware of our own propensity to fail at times. We try to extend toleration to the other. Sir Arthur Wing Pinero said, "It is only one step from toleration to forgiveness."

The process of reconciliation is one step backward and two steps forward. In our fantasies, progress is continuous and rapid, but in real life, progress is herky-jerky.

When reconciliation takes two steps forward, we try to practice an "attitude of gratitude." We notice progress by the other person. We say aloud what we notice. We thank the person for being willing to work toward reconciliation.

Failures of trustworthiness are alarm bells. If the other person hurts us, we don't sit on our hands awaiting an apology, but we approach with open arms, not closed fists. We look for ways to help the other person save face. If we transgress, we offer explanations that do not deny, justify, or excuse untrustworthy behavior. We apologize and make restitution. It isn't fair to place the burden of reconciliation on the back of the person who's been hurt. Instead, let us remember the wise saying of psychologist Jack Corazzini: "It's not so much what you did. It's what you do about what you did."

When people have had marital troubles, the renewed love between them can be as fragile as a spider's web. Davis and Ramona came to our marriage-enrichment workshop from the community. They had almost divorced over Ramona's overinvolvement in work. The children had flown from the nest five years earlier. Ramona threw herself headlong into a career she felt had been on hold during the years the kids were growing up. Even then, Davis had considered her "driven." He longed for the empty nest, so the couple could recapture the halcyon days of their early marriage. Ramona's increased time at work made him bitter.

They had attended counseling successfully and had begun to reconnect with each other. But their bonds were few and far between. When they saw the advertisement at their jobs about our enrichment group on forgiveness, they jumped at it.

When the two-weekend workshop was half over, Ramona canceled a date with Davis to work late. She was behind on paperwork. Davis was alarmed and felt betrayed. At the group, he brought up his sense of betrayal. Ramona told her side. She was contrite and reminded him that they'd gone to the movies the night before. The group helped Davis see how he could practice his attitude of gratitude for the dates they had and his attitude of latitude for the small "betrayal."

On the Border

In the 1980s, Watts, in south-central Los Angeles, was the scene of extreme violence between two youth gangs, the Bloods and the Crips. These gangs lived in nearby neighborhoods, and the warfare between the two groups caused numerous casualties among gang members and bystanders.

Between the two neighborhoods, Aqeela Sherrills lived in a smaller community. The members of the Bloods and Crips moved back and forth across Aqeela's neighborhood. Aqeela couldn't be blamed for wanting to escape that neighborhood. Escape he did. He went east to college. At college, he became convinced that he was created to make a difference in the neighborhood battles between the Bloods and Crips. So he returned to Los Angeles. In 1989, he began to organize members of his neighborhood to march into both the Bloods' and Crips' home ground with a message of reconciliation—peace for peace's sake.

"Both groups tolerated us," Aqeela said. "They allowed us to march. They even listened to our rhetoric. But nothing seemed to change.

"Eventually we met the football great Jim Brown." (Many remember Jim Brown for his role in the film *The Dirty Dozen*.) "Jim Brown allowed us to come to his house. We had the run of the place. He listened to our message and encouraged us to talk. He was a big brother for our group. For six months, he simply listened and accepted us.

"Over that period, Jim Brown developed his own vision of how changes might occur. One night, six months later, he shared it with our group. An organization called Amer-I-Can was born. Amer-I-Can aimed to steer young men toward positive goals." In Amer-I-Can, older, wiser men mentor younger men.

Aqeela and his group were swept up into Jim Brown's vision. They began to believe that they could make a difference. They could help broker peace. Aqeela and his brother Daude held a meeting to motivate the group to go directly to the Bloods and Crips and attempt to begin conversations that would lead to a truce and reconciliation between the gangs.

"Yes, we were worried. We literally were afraid for our lives," Aqeela said. "But I said to the group, 'We are on the border between the neighborhoods. We should be the ones who stand in the middle between the Bloods and Crips and bring the neighborhoods together.' By the end of the night, we decided to march into both territories and bring a message of reconciliation." The message eventually led to a "peace treaty," a truce between the Bloods and Crips. After much sacrifice on each side, it led to reconciliation.

Aqeela's is a story of two steps forward and one step back. He stepped back when he left Los Angeles for school in the east, but he stepped forward when he moved back to his neighborhood. He stepped forward again when he organized the group to try to make a difference in the neighborhood. He retreated when the group seemed to have no impact. He and his fellow group members retreated once again into the safety of meeting with Jim Brown. But through the vision of Jim Brown and the courage of the members of Aqeela's group, they stepped forward into the gap between the Bloods and Crips and contributed a vital part to the forging of that truce and later to the reconciliation of the neighborhoods.

Reconciliation almost never seems to move in a straight line. Sometimes we trip and fall; sometimes we become discouraged and want to retreat completely from the prospect of reconciling. Yet if we can persevere, sometimes we can forge a reconciliation that is accepting and respectful of the two sides and also brings them together into a relationship that was not possible before. Into that relationship, we must try to build devotion, the last plank across the Bridge to Reconciliation.

CHAPTER 10

Devotion

We are what we repeatedly do. Excellence, then, is not an act but a habit.

—ARISTOTLE

To reconcile is to do more than decide to reconcile, discuss transgressions, and detoxify the relationship from previous damage and harmful expectations. Those three planks get us only within arm's reach of the center of the Bridge to Reconciliation. We might even be able to leap across the great divide into reconciliation from there, but our foothold is likely precarious. To meet in the center requires that we build a final plank: devotion (Figure 10.1).

Plank 4, devotion, is built from four boards that fit tongue in groove. We must (1) resolve our grief over what we have lost, (2) build love through empathy, (3) decrease the negative, and (4) increase the positive. Look at Figure 10.1 to see what makes up devotion.

Reconciliation is restoring trust where trust has been lost. We grieve what we've lost. Whether you lose a person or something less tangible (such as trust), you can grieve your loss in ways that

FIGURE 10.1
A Close-up of the
Underside of Devotion

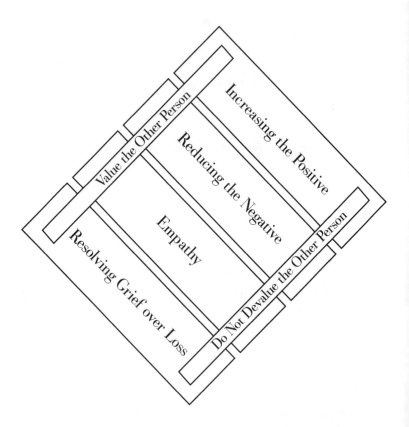

hamper or help your future adjustment. If you ignore the loss of trust, you'll continue to have doubts about the future of the relationship. To cover over the loss with a veneer of smiles would leave the wounds beneath the surface untended. Most people want to resolve the loss of trust with a new commitment. That requires an effective resolution to the grief.

Resolving Grief

Whether we are forgiving or unforgiving strongly affects how we'll grieve and our character after we have grieved. I saw the connection between forgiveness and grief as I mourned my mother's death. You have seen the story of my forgiveness for her murderer unfold throughout the book, but the story wouldn't be complete without describing how I grieved her death.

THE STAGES OF GRIEF

For two weeks after finding out about my mother's murder, my emotions were in turmoil. I went through the funeral and murder investigation on autopilot. Emotions popped up unexpectedly. Sadness—I missed her. Guilt—I should have phoned more often. Fear—I'm a forty-eight-year-old orphan; what does that mean for me?

Returning home to Richmond, I withdrew into a protective shell. I poked my head out only to talk with Kirby. I deflected discussions about my feelings.

My first two weeks were consistent with findings from scientific studies of grieving. The beginning of grief is usually a period of emotional turmoil and vulnerability.

The beginning of grief is usually a period of emotional turmoil and vulnerability.

When we grieve, we typically tell a story over and over in our minds about our relationship with the person we've lost. We might think, *If only I had made my loved one wear a seat belt, he wouldn't have been killed in the accident.* In reality, we probably never would have been able to make him wear a seat belt. We had no possible

control over whether he wore a seat belt. But "if only . . ." thinking is the core of the obsessive mental review we undertake as we
grieve. We think about our story at night. Events unexpectedly
trigger memories. As we retell the story, it evolves. A detail changes
here, another detail the next time.

At the same time, we seem compelled to tell others the story of
the loss. If you have been on the receiving end of these stories, you
know how frustrating it can be. A friend describes her childhood
relations with her recently departed father. You sympathize. The
next day she tells the same story. You sympathize again. The day
after that, it's still the same story. By the fifth time, only your essential humanity prevents you from shouting, "Get over it! Get a
life!" You want to scream and pull out your hair. By the tenth
time, you don't want to see the person. She'll just tell the story
again. This is compulsive social review. It's a normal part of grief,
but it's tough on friendships.

I was a textbook case. I knew about compulsive social review,
and I didn't want to drive my friends and family crazy. So I didn't
talk much about my grief to them. I'm sure they were relieved.
However, I told the story of my mother's murder and of my experience at forgiving repeatedly in my public talks.

After I had told the story five times or so, though, I started to
chastise myself. *I don't need to tell about Mom at this conference,* I
would say to myself. But when the conference was in full swing,
in the midst of my talk, I would tell the story anyway. That com-
pulsion lasted for almost a year after my mother's death. At the
time, I didn't understand why I kept telling the story. I thought
that perhaps I'd developed a morbid fascination with her death. I
hadn't. It was simple grief. I was doing exactly what I needed to do
to get over her death.

Why do we obsessively think about and compulsively tell others the story of our loss? Because we are working hard to make sense out of our life without the loved one. We are seeking a story that makes sense. At first, the story doesn't quite fit, but as we tell it over and over, it evolves. One day, *voilà!* The story makes sense—not in a logical way, but in an emotional way. Perhaps after six months, perhaps a year, maybe two, our obsession with figuring out the meaning of a loss ceases. We become at peace with our story.

Whether we forgive or don't is crucial to the final story we tell ourselves and others. Whether we forgive or don't also helps shape our character after we resolve the grief. Suppose we're grieving the loss of love in a romantic relationship, whether we're headed toward divorce, have been jilted, or simply feel trapped in a cold, passionless relationship. During grieving, we constantly review our story. If we are unforgiving, the story is filled with rumination about unfairness, bitterness, hatred, rage, hostility, and resentment. We are obsessed with unforgiveness. We compulsively share our bitter story with our family and friends.

> *Whether we forgive or don't is crucial to the final story we tell ourselves and others. Whether we forgive or don't also helps shape our character after we resolve the grief.*

This has two effects. First, we program into our brain a story of bitterness and unforgiveness that will take years to undo. It transforms our personality, making us bitter, unforgiving people. Second, we strain our friendships. When we tell a story of unforgiveness repeatedly, friends and family support us for a while.

They know that we've suffered. Yet their tolerance for hearing bitter, hateful, resentful stories is limited. We drive away the very people we need by compulsively telling unforgiving stories.

On the other hand, if we forgive from the heart quickly, we grieve differently. Our obsessive thoughts are filled with empathy, compassion, sympathy, and love. We picture ourselves as being forgiving. We feel compassion. We visualize ourselves, within the midst of one of the most difficult personal experiences that people can have, as showing positive character traits.

If we forgive deeply but quickly, we tell others a more balanced story, not a false story that says, "I never thought anything bad of this youth who killed my mother. I condone this crime against me." False forgiveness is syrupy and unbelievable. It extracts its price from our social network. It makes friends want to spit out the saccharine sweetness. It doesn't attract the social support we need. Rather, real forgiveness says, "A genuine wrong was done. I could choose to hate him for what he did to me. Instead, I choose to understand. I see him as a human, not merely an object of my hatred, not merely a betrayer of trust." That story typically goes down better with friends and is more nourishing for our character.

Grieving ends when we come to a resolution with the story about the loss. We finally arrive at a life narrative that lets us understand at a deep level a plot in which we are the central character. Forgiveness is the twist in the plot that allows us to tell a story that helps us move forward. Unforgiveness is either an unfinished story or one we never want to revisit. I have summarized the roles of unforgiveness and forgiveness in grieving in Table 10.1.

GRIEVING MY LOSS OF REPUTATION

I'm sometimes ashamed of the petty hurts that happen in academic life. Yet that world is where I live much of the time.

TABLE 10.1

The Roles of Unforgiveness and Forgiveness in Grieving

Stage	Numbed Shock	OBSESSIVE THOUGHT, COMPULSIVE TALK		Resolution
		Obsessive Mental Review	Compulsive Social Review	
Story	Ripples of shock cause our story of life to disintegrate. What will life be like without this person or relationship?	We retell the story repeatedly in our minds, trying to formulate a new understanding. Small changes happen with retelling.	We retell the story repeatedly to others trying to formulate a new understanding. Small changes happen with retelling.	We settle on a new story of how life will be. This includes changes in our self-concept and in our network of supporters.
Role of Unforgiveness	Initial emotions lay the groundwork for the development of unforgiveness.	If we mentally rehearse unforgiving thoughts and emotions, we feed a self-concept as bitter, resentful, and angry.	If we socially rehearse unforgiving stories, we strain friendships and turn the tone of the relationship negative.	We can harden our self-concept as unforgiving and drive away friends.
Role of Forgiveness	Forgiveness can replace initial emotions and prevent unforgiveness from ever developing.	If we mentally rehearse forgiving thoughts, we feed a self-concept as empathic, forgiving, and compassionate.	If we socially rehearse forgiving stories, we do not add negativity to the demands already on friends to listen and support.	We can create a firm self-concept as forgiving and maintain a positive support network.

It was early in my career. One of the students whose work I had supervised was defending his master's thesis. In those meetings, the student presents his or her written thesis to a committee of professors and observers. He describes the research and answers questions posed by the professors. In this case, the defense was not going well. One professor was being particularly hard on the student, who was struggling.

At the end of the painful meeting, the student is always asked to step outside while the committee decides whether he or she passed or failed. Students who pass are assigned a grade of A or B. Almost all students receive a grade of A.

As the doorway swung shut, the "difficult" professor erupted. "This is inferior work," he blasted.

Another professor chimed in, "I thought the student wrote well and gave a good talk." He turned to the "difficult" professor and said, "What did you find to be so disturbing?"

"The student missed a whole line of research on the topic. It wasn't even mentioned. In my lab, I've studied this topic for five years in at least ten studies."

I felt my stomach sink. I hadn't thought to direct my student toward that professor's research. The "difficult" professor looked directly at me. "I'll pass the thesis with a B because I don't expect a student to know better. But the person who really deserves the B is you, Ev."

I could feel my face flush. Of course, he was right. I had blundered. I was shamed by the public critique.

Over the next weeks, I grieved my loss of reputation. Psychology departments are small communities. Word got around fast. I was sad and mad. I began to ruminate. I didn't want to look the "difficult" professor in the eye. I fussed and fumed as Kirby and I went on nightly walks.

Maybe six months later, I realized that unforgiveness and un-resolved grief were poisoning me. The "difficult" professor seemed to have forgotten the event. It was just another thesis defense in his long academic career. I could see how offended he must have been that I hadn't remembered his research even though we worked together daily.

Finally, I forgave him for his shaming critique. I accepted the event as a painful learning experience. I grieved the loss of my reputation. In the end, I saw myself as an inexperienced professor. I wasn't perfect. I could learn. I could forgive when I was shamed for my mistakes. That story helped me move on and let me later approach the professor and reconcile with him.

To reconcile requires that we grieve whatever we feel we have lost. Forgiveness helps resolve the grief in a way that allows us to move toward love.

To reconcile requires that we grieve whatever we feel we have lost.

Building Love

WHAT IS LOVE?

We usually think of love as romantic love or love of family. I recommend a broader definition. Love is being willing to value people and unwilling to devalue them. Love can be built in any relationship. To complete the Bridge to Reconciliation, we set our goal as valuing the person who hurt or offended us. First, we must understand how the person would perceive love. We try to understand how he or she would feel valued. To avoid devaluing the person, we try to understand what acts he or she would perceive as devaluing. Then we try, as much as it depends on us, to increase the positive and decrease the negative interactions between us. As John Gottman's research reveals, good relationships usually have a ratio of positives to negatives of at least five to one.

Love is being willing to value people and unwilling to devalue them.

DETERMINE WHAT THE OTHER PERSON WOULD PERCEIVE TO BE LOVE

When Kirby and I were first married, we sometimes misunderstood each other's acts of love. Typically, I would come into the kitchen, where she was cooking dinner. I would put my arms around her, hug her close, and perhaps give her an affectionate squeeze and caress. She would squirm away, say, "I love you," and go back to cooking. I would grunt and move away. Both of us were unsatisfied.

In thinking back to our histories, it's easy now for me to see what was happening. I was reared in a home where we didn't talk about love. Dad wasn't as nonverbal as the husband who said, "I told her I loved her when we were married, and I'll let her know if things change." But he came close. My mother and father were physically affectionate with each other, and I have vivid pictures of my dad squeezing my mom, surprising her with a kiss on the back of the neck, or giving her an affectionate pat on the bottom as she leaned over. I learned by watching that a husband shows love through physical touch and affection.

When I visited Kirby's family for the first time, however, I saw strange happenings I had a hard time understanding. Before we even got into the house, one member or another of Kirby's family was professing love to another. I left after a brief visit feeling like

I'd never heard the phrase "I love you" used so many times in such a short period. Kirby had learned to show love by saying it.

In our early months of marriage, we each attempted to put the Golden Rule into practice: Do unto others as you would have them do unto you. I showed Kirby love through physical affection, and Kirby told me repeatedly how much she loved me. But I wasn't getting enough physical affection, and Kirby wasn't hearing "I love you" as often as she longed to. *All she wants to do is talk about it,* I thought. *Ev just wants to paw me twenty-four hours a day,* she thought. I really wanted Kirby to understand how I could perceive love (through physical affection) and for her to show me in that way. She really wanted me to tell her, "I love you." We changed our ways. Now, thirty years later, Kirby's all over me. I tell her "I love you" a lot. We both smile much more often.

Popular writer Gary Chapman in his book *Five Languages of Love* identified five ways that people like to have love shown to them. We've already mentioned words of love and encouragement (Kirby's primary love language) and physical touch and affection (mine). For others, spending quality time together is a love language. Quality time includes talking about things that both consider important or doing things together that both enjoy. Acts of loving service—such as when one does something nice, gets meals ready, or helps with a burdensome chore—are ways people show love. For some, gifts convey love. Knowing that a loved one has spent time and money selecting the perfect gift is evidence of thoughtfulness, love, and valuing. In sum, to build love, we first identify how a person perceives love and then show love in that way.

While Chapman's five languages of love are not the only ways that people can show love, they are among the most common. To understand how to show love, rank the five languages of love as you think your spouse, children, or friends would rank them. Then ask each person if your list fits them. The person might have a different perception and help you understand himself or herself more accurately.

Even in relationships outside the home, you can use the languages of love. At work, for example, some colleagues like to be encouraged verbally, while others feel that such encouragement is patronizing. Some colleagues enjoy a pat on the back. Others don't want to be touched. Some colleagues enjoy spending quality time with coworkers. Others limit their nonwork socializing to family relations and relations outside of work. Some colleagues enjoy your doing acts of service for them. Others feel that your service for them communicates that you don't trust or respect them ("What, she doesn't think I can do it myself?"). Some colleagues enjoy receiving gifts of appreciation. Others look upon this with suspicion and distrust. Analyzing your workplace can help determine what language of love to use if those relationships need repair.

DECREASING NEGATIVE INTERACTIONS

As we've discussed, when a relationship is troubled, the ratio of positive to negative interactions between the people is usually well below five to one. Let's assume the ratio is one to one. For every ten positive interactions, two people have ten negative interactions on an average day. The fastest way to change this ratio, moving it closer to the ideal of five to one (or more), is to decrease the number of negative interactions. For example, if the partners who had the one-to-one ratio were to decrease negative interactions by a mere eight, the ratio would be five to one. In order to change the ratio to five to one by increasing positive interactions, however, they would have to have forty *additional* positive interactions each day. To make rapid changes in a negative relationship, first try to decrease the negative.

INCREASING POSITIVE INTERACTIONS

On the other hand, there are many problems associated with decreasing negative interactions. For one, it's difficult to get the other person to notice what you're *not* doing.

Suppose you and I are in a negative relationship. I feel the urge to criticize you, but I refrain from doing that. You won't notice anything different. You won't know that I'm actively trying to make the relationship better. We'll end the day feeling more positive toward each other because we have had fewer negative interactions, but you won't perceive that I'm trying to change. Therefore, you might attribute the change to the weather or to your own attempts to make the relationship more positive.

On the other hand, if I do positive acts that I know you'll like, you'll notice. Those acts are so positive and perhaps unexpected, they'll stand out. You'll see that I'm making a good effort. The problem is, I must do forty of those to make a difference.

Obviously, if we want to change the ratio fast and powerfully, we need to do both: decrease the negative *and* increase the positive. Think of love like money. If I do a loving act, that places one love dollar in our love bank. If I do a negative act, however, it removes five love dollars. (This is an adaptation of a metaphor used by Willard Harley Jr. in his books *His Needs, Her Needs,* and *Love Busters.*) Based on your understanding of the other person's love language, try to increase your deposits to the person's account while decreasing the withdrawals.

Reconciliation During a Family Squabble

Yesterday I overheard a conversation between my wife and seventeen-year-old daughter, Katy Anna. The conversation began innocently enough, with my daughter's announcement that she intended to go with her cousin Carol to downtown Richmond to advise Carol on purchasing a dress for the senior homecoming dance. Kirby was surprised. She said that she didn't think that the trip was a good idea because Katy Anna hadn't done some of her chores, which she'd promised to do during the week. She hadn't cleaned her room, packaged some books to send away, or written thank-you letters for some gifts.

"I'll do those this afternoon or tomorrow," said Katy Anna.

"You said that earlier in the week," ventured Kirby. "The chores are still not done."

You can probably imagine the flow of this conversation. It progressed along what one might expect would be normal parent-adolescent lines. Kirby kept insisting that the work needed to be done because it was the responsible thing to do. She encouraged Katy Anna to put off her pleasure until she had done her work. Katy Anna, on the other hand, kept pointing to times when she *had* been responsible. She enumerated several times when she'd done her work and also socialized with her friends.

Such discussions are filled with high emotion and tension on both sides. Fortunately in our home, these occur very infrequently. Nevertheless, my stomach was tight just overhearing the conversation.

I was keeping a low profile. (You can call this wisdom or—probably more accurate—being chicken.) As I listened, I was so proud of my family. Kirby kept asking Katy Anna what she was feeling and thinking. Kirby has always been an encouraging listener, and even though the interaction was difficult, she encouraged Katy Anna multiple times to share her feelings.

Katy Anna also was behaving with great maturity. Instead of getting angry and sullen and clamming up, as many teenagers do, she was able to hang in there and explain her feelings. "I feel like I have many more rules than most of my friends," she said. "I see my older sisters and brother having much more freedom than I do. I realize that they're older than I am, but it's hard being the youngest child."

Kirby would reflect back Katy Anna's frustration and continue to affirm that she understood Katy Anna's struggle. Kirby also explained that in her heart was the desire to help Katy Anna develop maturity. Katy Anna acknowledged Kirby's care and concern.

After probably thirty minutes of discussion, they worked out an agreement. As the listener, I couldn't help but be amazed at the love they showed for each other as well as the mutual respect that they communicated. Reconciliation is all about deciding to talk, talking softly in love, empathizing, repairing any hurt feelings (sooner rather than later), and building a sense of loving devotion that both people feel.

Susan

Remember Susan from Chapter 6? She worked through the Pyramid Model to REACH Forgiveness and fully forgave her father, who had been diagnosed with prostate cancer. She was able to turn loose fifteen years of unforgiveness by vividly imagining forgiveness for one symbolic act—the Friendly's episode in which her father embarrassed her in front of her friends.

Still, the prospect of facing the old man made her stomach knot. She wasn't sure the relationship would work out. As it turned out, things didn't go as she had planned. Let's walk over the Bridge to Reconciliation with Susan as a review.

Susan weighed the questions about reconciliation. Should she visit him? What would he be like? Would he be as gruff and preoccupied as he'd always been? Susan didn't even know how to empathize accurately. After fifteen years of noncontact, she was out of the habit of worrying about him and what he thought.

"What if he dies and we've never even talked?" she asked her best friend, Marta.

Marta stirred her coffee thoughtfully. "You've lived without him for fifteen years. You'll probably feel bad for a while." Marta took a sip. "But you'll survive."

"Marta, you're always so philosophical. I don't want merely to survive."

"Yeah, I know. You think that because you've forgiven him, you can suddenly make everything right just by showing up. Well, you're my good friend and I don't want to see you hurt."

"I don't think I'll get hurt," said Susan.

"You always say that, but this guy hasn't changed. He's the same insensitive jerk who pulled you out of Friendly's that time back in high school. You're setting yourself up for getting wiped out."

"I want to try," said Susan. "I'm not going to bring up the past if he doesn't. I'll just visit and see how things develop."

"Yeah, right. They'll develop."

Susan was nervous as she phoned. "He's not here," a gravelly male voice answered her query. "He'll be back about six. Why don't you come then? Or maybe after supper?"

"Do you think he'll mind if I just show up?"

"No problem. I know he'll be here. We eat about six-thirty.

Come before or after." Susan nervously scribbled the address and directions. It was not a high-rent district.

Susan thought about the benefits of a time-limited visit. "I'll come by around six."

The place is a dump, thought Susan as she parked her blue Ford Taurus out front precisely at six o'clock. The sign by the doorbell said Out of Harm's Way. She punched the bell.

The door opened to a man in his late thirties, brown beard, jeans, and T-shirt advertising Diet Pepsi.

"I phoned earlier, uh . . ."

"About Ted, right?" The voice was older than the face appeared to be. "He's on the third floor in three-B."

"Uh, what is this place? An apartment building, or what?"

"It's a recovery house for alcoholics. We help each other."

Great, Susan thought as she made her way up the two flights of stairs. She took a deep breath at the top. She found 3B on the right side of the hall.

Her father's eyes in a withered face came into view as the door opened to her knock. "Susie," he said, stepping backward and letting the door swing inward.

"Susan," she corrected. "Everyone calls me Susan now."

"Well, you'll still be Susie to me," he said sharply. "Anyway, come in."

The one-room apartment was dominated by a rumpled, unmade bed. Susan's father gestured at a dirt-colored, once-plaid recliner. "Chair?"

They settled in—Susan's father at the chair by a wooden table, Susan in the recliner.

"How are you?" she ventured.

"Been better," he said.

You're not making this easy for me, she thought.

"I don't need sympathy," he added.

Susan started to shoot back a retort. She paused. "I know," she said.

"I expect you got the message that I have prostate cancer."

"I did. Hazel Hendrick phoned me."

"Ran into her at the hospital. She was visiting. I was getting checked to see if I was fit for surgery. I told her to tell you if she ever saw you."

"How bad is the cancer?"

"They don't think it's worthwhile to operate. It's already in my system. Just a matter of time. Stage four, they say."

"Dad, I'm sorry."

"No, you aren't, Susie. I gave you a hard time growing up and you gave me a hard time. I think that not speaking for fifteen years is pretty clear evidence that you aren't sorry."

Susan looked down. "I wasn't very mature. I'm older and, I hope, wiser now."

"We're both older," he said. "I wanted to at least say good-bye. I guess I didn't want to leave you with all bad memories."

"I have tried to forgive you, and . . . I understand that I was a handful too. I'm sorry. I hope you can forgive me."

"So you *tried* to forgive me. Does that mean you couldn't?"

"I did, and do, forgive you."

"I wasn't much of a dad to you. Then after your mom died, the social drinking got out of hand. After a couple of years, I got into treatment. Then I came here."

"Dad, I hate to see you living here. Can I do something? Give you some money so you can move? Can I help?"

"Susie, I told you I don't need sympathy. In fact, I *choose* to live here. I actually support this house financially."

"You do?"

"Yeah. I always worked hard. I saved over a million in stocks. When I became an alcoholic, this house and these people helped me. So when I got back on my feet, I started to help the house. I set up an endowment of a half million. It provides enough in interest to keep the house going. It will after I'm gone as well."

"I'm touched," said Susan.

"I wanted to tell you face-to-face that I'm leaving you the money I have left, except for that endowment. I know that money won't buy back the years we missed, but maybe it's a start at making up. Can you accept the money as a late gift from a dying old man?"

Susan felt a tear run down her cheek. She nodded.

"Thanks. You've made me happier . . ." He paused, and Susan looked up. ". . . Susan."

Overcoming Obstacles to Reconciliation

At this point in the young history of the scientific study of forgiveness and reconciliation, we don't know how to get around or climb over all the obstacles to reconciliation. Through both our and others' scientific studies, we are finding out more about how to help people forgive faster and more thoroughly and reconcile in ways that are more lasting.

I recall a classic Gary Larson cartoon in which two scientists are standing in front of a blackboard filled from top left to bottom right with equations. In the middle is one blank line with a dotted line connecting the top and bottom half of the equations. Beside the line is printed, "About here a miracle occurs." One scientist says, "Do you think we need to be a little more explicit about that?"

I have tried to be more explicit about this miracle of forgiveness and reconciliation throughout this book. Forgiveness is not a panacea. Along with social justice, a system of laws, a method of resolving differences, and an intentional effort to reconcile, it is one strand of Blake's Golden String:

> *I give to you the end of a Golden String*
> *Only wind it into a ball*
> *And it will lead you in to Heaven's Gate*
> *Set in Jerusalem's Wall.*

I have tried to help you grasp that string when you struggle to find it, so you can wind it close to your heart.

The Limits of a Science of Forgiveness

I have described some of the findings from our scientific study of unforgiveness and forgiveness. We have discovered ways that help people move through the Pyramid Model to REACH Forgiveness. We have found how to pause on the Bridge to Reconciliation to decide whether, when, and how to reconcile, to discuss transgressions softly, to detoxify the poison in the relationship, and to build devotion. We have learned a method of explicit reconciliation that guides us plank by plank into a meeting in the center of the bridge.

Our scientific findings help explain much wisdom drawn from writers in the humanities and theology. I have illustrated some of this wisdom in quotes scattered throughout the text and at the beginning of each chapter.

We now better understand that forgiveness is rooted in other-oriented love. In the end, though, a science of forgiveness, even when coupled with knowledge of forgiveness from theology and the humanities, can take us only so far. There is a long plunge from a hurt and unforgiving heart into the refreshing water of a heart at rest in forgiveness. Knowledge won't make us jump. We can stand at the brink knowing how to forgive but be unwilling to jump. In the classic movie *Butch Cassidy and the Sundance Kid,* Butch (Paul Newman) and Sundance (Robert Redford) were pinned down by bounty hunters who chased them with the tenacity of the Energizer bunny. Escape required them to jump into a river far below them.

"Let's jump," says Butch.

"Nope," says Sundance, drawing his pistol. "We'll fight."

"We'll be killed."

"Yep, but we'll fight."

Often we take that stance rather than risk forgiving. Sundance won't jump because he can't swim. "Hell, the fall will probably kill you," says Butch encouragingly.

There was nothing else to do. The force of Butch's courage encouraged Sundance to take the plunge. It was risky. It was hard to do. But they plunged in, floating the river together, and were free.

Thomas Paine, one of the founders of freedom in the United States, said, "That which we obtain too easily, we esteem too lightly." Opening ourselves to granting other-oriented forgiveness isn't easy. No friend, family member, author, or television personality can do it for us. We each control the doorway to forgiving. When we allow that door to open, we step through it and leap outward to plunge into cool, refreshing freedom. Perhaps just as important, we also encourage and bless the other person with the gift of forgiving that is for giving.

NOTES

Introduction

WHY FORGIVE?

1 McCullough, M. E., Sandage, S. J., and Worthington, E. L., Jr. (1997). *To forgive is human: How to put your past in the past.* Downers Grove, IL: InterVarsity Press. This book is available through IVP directly at 800-843-9487 or through www.amazon.com.

2 Carrier, Christopher (May 2000). "From darkness to light." *Reader's Digest,* 101–106.

Chapter 1

LAYING THE FOUNDATION

1 Worthington, Everett L., Jr. (2000). "Is there a place for forgiveness in the justice system?" *Fordham Urban Law Journal, 27,* 1721–1734.

2 Damasio, Antonio R. (1994). *Descartes' error: Emotion, reason, and the human brain.* New York: Avon Books.

Chapter 2

R: RECALL THE HURT

1 Cox, Deborah, Stabb, Sally, and Bruchner, Karin (1999). *Women's anger: Clinical and developmental perspectives.* New York: Brunner/Mazel, pp. 102–103.

Chapter 3

E: EMPATHIZE

1 Levenson, R. W., and Ruef, A. M. (1992). "Empathy: A physiological substrate." *Journal of Personality and Social Psychology, 63,* 234–246.

2 Malcolm, Wanda M., and Greenberg, Leslie S. (2000). "Forgiveness as a process of change in psychotherapy." In Michael E. McCullough, Kenneth I. Pargament, and Carl E. Thoresen (eds.), *Forgiveness: Theory, research, and practice.* New York: Guilford Press, pp.179–202.

3 Milgram, Stanley (1974). *Obedience to authority.* New York: Harper & Row.

Chapter 4

A: ALTRUISTIC GIFT OF FORGIVENESS

1 Murray, Andrew (1997). *Humility: The beauty of holiness.* Old Tappan, NJ: Fleming Revel.

2 Chacour, E., and Hazard, David. (1984). *Blood brothers: A palestinian struggles for reconciliation in the Middle East.* New York: Chosen Books.

Chapter 5

C: COMMIT PUBLICLY TO FORGIVE

1 Marks, Richard D. (1999). "Firststone: A biblical forgiveness intervention for pastors and christian counselors." *Marriage and Family: A Christian Journal, 2,* 307–312.

2 Pennebaker, J. W. (ed.) (1995). *Emotion, disclosure, and health.* Washington, D.C.: American Psychological Association Press.

Chapter 6

H: HOLD ON TO FORGIVENESS

1 Wegner, Daniel (1994). *White bears and other unwanted thoughts: Suppression, obsession, and the psychology of mental control.* New York: Guilford Press.

2 Mischel, Walter, and Mischel, H. N. (1976). "A cognitive social learning approach to morality and self-regulation." In T. Lickona (ed.), *Moral development and behavior: Theory, research, and social issues.* New York: Holt, Rinehart and Winston.

3 Baumeister, Roy F., and Exline, Julie Juola (2000). "Self-control, morality, and human strength." *Journal of Social and Clinical Psychology, 19,* 29–42.

Chapter 7

DECISIONS

1 Worthington, E. L., Jr., and Drinkard, D. T. (2000). "Promoting reconciliation through psychoeducational and therapeutic interventions." *Journal of Marital and Family Therapy, 26,* 93–101.

2 Worthington, E. L., Jr., and Wade, N. G. (1999). "The social psychology of unforgiveness and forgiveness and implications for clinical practice." *Journal of Social and Clinical Psychology, 18,* 385–418.

3 deWaal, Frans (1989). *Chimpanzee politics: Power and sex among apes.* Baltimore: The John Hopkins University Press.

Chapter 8

DISCUSSION

1 Jones, L. Gregory (1995). *Embodying forgiveness: A theological analysis.* Grand Rapids, MI: William B. Eerdmans Company.

2 Stillwell, A. M., and Baumeister, Roy F. (1997). "The construction of victim and perpetrator memories: Accuracy and distortion in role-based accounts." *Personality and Social Psychology Bulletin, 23,* 1157–1172.

3 Sandage, S. J., Worthington, E. L., Jr., Hight, T. L., and Berry, J. W. (2000). "Seeking forgiveness: Theoretical context and an initial empirical study." *Journal of Psychology and Theology, 28,* 21–35.

4 Tangney, June Price (2000). "Humility: Theoretical perspectives, empirical findings and directions for future research." *Journal of Social and Clinical Psychology, 19,* 70–82.

Chapter 9

DETOXIFICATION

1 Gottman, John Mordechai (1994). *Why marriages succeed or fail . . . and how you can make yours last.* New York: Simon & Schuster.

INDEX

ABOUT THE AUTHOR

EVERETT WORTHINGTON, PH.D., is professor and chair of psychology at Virginia Commonwealth University. He is executive director of A Campaign for Forgiveness Research, which, in collaboration with the John Templeton Foundation, has raised funding for more than thirty-five research projects studying forgiveness. He is an active leader in secular and Christian counseling fields and has appeared on CNN, *Good Morning America,* and other national shows. He lives in Richmond, Virginia.